بسم الله الرحمن الرحيم

الصلاة والسلام عليك يا رسول الله

Modesty in Islam

Compiled By:

Maulana Mohammed Shakir Noorie

(Ameer – Sunni Dawat e Islami)

Translated by:

Muhammed Salim Noorie

Presented by: Idarah Ma'arif e Islami

Published by: Maktab e Taibah

Book Name: Modesty in Islam

Compiled By: Maulana Mohammed Shakir Noorie
(Ameer – Sunni Dawat e Islami)

Translation: Muhammed Salim Noorie (Canada)

Proofreading: Mohammed Noorani Mohmed Noorie (U.K.), Fatimah Zehra Patel (U.K.)

Cover: Mohammed Rauf Patel (India)

Presented By: Idarah Ma'arif e Islami

Published By: Maktab e Taibah, 126 Kambekar St, Mumbai.

PUBLISHED BY: MAKTAB E TAIBAH

WORLDWIDE HEADQUARTERS
ISMAIL HABIB MASJID | 126 KAMBEKAR ST
MUMBAI 3 | 0091 22 23434366
WWW.SUNNIDAWATEISLAMI.NET

UK BRANCH
MARKAZ SDI | NOOR MASJID | NOOR ST
PRESTON | PR1 1QS | (0044) 01772 881786

ISBN 978-0-9935735-2-1

CONTENTS

Dedicated To:

The most beloved daughter of the Prophet ﷺ,
Queen of the Worlds, Embodiment of Purity and Modesty,
Leader of the Ladies of Paradise,
Sayyidah Fāṭimah al-Zahrā ...

Every moment of her chaste and virtuous life is a shining example for Muslim women everywhere.

بِسْمِ اللّٰهِ الرَّحْمٰنِ الرَّحِيْمِ

اَلصَّلٰوةُ وَالسَّلَامُ عَلَيْكَ يَا رَسُوْلَ اللّٰهِ ﷺ

Introduction

Modesty is a great human quality with a number of other beautiful qualities taking root in a person who has modesty. A modest person becomes attracted to goodness, avoids evil at all times and begins to love all things and all work associated with goodness. On the other hand, one who has no shame or modesty does not see the difference between good and bad. This is indicated in the following Ḥadīth:

اِذَا لَمْ تَسْتَحْيِ فَافْعَلْ مَا شِئْتَ

If you feel no shame, then do as you wish.

(Musnad Imām Aḥmad, Chapter 38, Pg. 433)

Today, when modesty and shame are being destroyed by electronic and print media; honour is being trampled upon and morals and characters are being destroyed, it is essential for us, more than ever, to talk about modesty. It is modesty that encourages a person towards all goodness and stops a person from all evils. It is the pinnacle of good character, the adornment of belief and the beauty of Islām. It would not be wrong to say that modesty is the voice of human nature. The importance, merits and necessity of modesty is such a topic that it needs many books just to introduce the subject. However, our beloved Prophet ﷺ has explained it in such a beautiful and condensed manner with an ocean of knowledge in this short sentence. Sayyidunā Abū Hurairah ؓ narrates that the Prophet ﷺ said:

اَلْاِيْمَانُ بِضْعٌ وَّسِتُّوْنَ شُعْبَةً وَّالْحَيَآءُ شُعْبَةٌ مِّنَ الْاِيْمَانِ

Faith consists of more than sixty branches and modesty is a branch of faith.

(Ṣaḥīḥ al-Bukhārī, Vol. 1, Pg. 11)

This narration has also been reported with slight variations. In some narrations the number 'seventy' is used in place of 'sixty'. In any case, this narration tells us that from all the qualities which complete a person's faith, modesty is one of them. The question arises, 'Why is modesty declared to be a branch of faith?' The answer is that modesty and faith (belief) both invite a person towards goodness and keep a person associated with goodness; which in turn, also stop and keep a person far away from evil at all times.

We learn from this narration that faith and modesty have a very close mutual relationship. This means that a person who is a sincere believer will also be modest. Where you see a lack of modesty and shame, know that there will be an equivalent lack of faith and belief in that person.

Modesty has great importance in Islām and without it, a person cannot be a complete believer. According to Islām, modesty is an important human quality which raises the status and majesty of one who possesses modesty and shame. On the other hand, according to a large number of people, modesty is an illness. It is for this reason that the West has proclaimed the slogan 'Shyness is a Sickness.' They consider it to be an illness and even use medication in order to overcome it. One of the larger differences between Muslims and other religions is that Islamic teachings consider modesty to be a golden trait whilst other religions have no real concept of modesty in their teachings. In many cases, they do not think twice about making shamelessness a part of their teachings.

Indecency and evil have become very common in our societies nowadays. It is an era of fashion and modernism. Our Muslim brothers and sisters are forsaking Islamic teachings and principles and adopting Western values and cultures. Muslims are also taking part in indecency and nudity. In such a delicate and difficult environment, it is even more important to make Muslims aware of the dangers of evil and indecency. It is for this reason that this book has been compiled. In putting together this book, great help was received from Maulana Syed Imranuddin Najmi and Maulana Abdullah Azmi Najmi (Teachers, Jamia Hira, Mahapoli). Additionally, Gulam Mustafa Agha (Student, Jamia Hira, Mahapoli) helped with the composing. May Allāh ﷻ reward them all according to His status and means and accept this small effort we have made. May He make this a means of reforming the Muslim Ummah, Āmīn.

Dust at the feet of the Pious

Mohammed Shakir Noorie

12th Muharram al-Haram 1438

بِسْمِ اللّٰهِ الرَّحْمٰنِ الرَّحِيْمِ

اَلصَّلٰوةُ وَالسَّلَامُ عَلَيْكَ يَا رَسُوْلَ اللّٰهِ ﷺ

Humans beings are the best of all creations and have superiority over all other creations. Allāh ﷻ has placed many beautiful qualities in humans and one such quality is modesty/shyness. It is a result of this modesty that a person avoids sins and is attracted towards good deeds. Indecency and immodesty leads to a person becoming trapped in a spiral of disobedience and sins.

Meaning and Explanation of Modesty

"اَلْحَيَاءُ" (Al-Ḥayā-u) *has an elongated (stretched) 'Alif', which is derived from the word 'Al-Ḥayāt'. It is also the root for the word 'Al-Ḥaya' with a shortened 'Alif'. The more that the heart of a community is alive, the more modesty will be found in it. Lack of modesty is a sign of a dead heart and soul. The amount of modesty in a person or community is directly linked to how alive the heart is."* (Subul al-Hudā wa al-Rashad)

Experts of terminology describe it in the following manner:

تَغَيُّرٌ وَّانْكِسَارٌ يَّعْتَرِىْ لِلْاِنْسَانِ مِنْ خَوْفِ مَا يُعَابُ بِهٖ

Modesty is the feeling that when it is present in a person, it prevents him from carrying out faulty deeds.

(Al-Qāmūs al-Fiqhī, Vol. 1, Pg. 109)

Religious experts have described it as follows:

خُلُقٌ يَّبْعَثُ عَلَى اجْتِنَابِ الْقَبِيْحِ، وَيَمْنَعُ مِنَ التَّقْصِيْرِ فِيْ حَقِّ ذِي الْحَقِّ

Modesty is a characteristic which prevents a person from evil things and stops a person from stepping on the rights of others.

(Ibid)

Imām Rāghib al-Aṣfahānī رحمه الله writes:

'Modesty is a quality which restrains a person from committing evil deeds. According to a great number of scholars, modesty is the thing which encourages a person to do good and avoid evil.'

There are a number of other narrations reported about the meaning and description of modesty, however, they all state that it prevents the heart from carrying out evil acts or deeds.

Modesty is a Quality of Allāh ﷻ

According to Aḥādīth, modesty is one of the blessed Attributes of Allāh ﷻ. Ḥaḍrat Salmān رضي الله عنه narrates that the Prophet ﷺ said:

إِنَّ رَبَّكُمْ حَيِيٌّ كَرِيمٌ، يَسْتَحْيِي مِنْ عَبْدِهِ أَنْ يَرْفَعَ إِلَيْهِ يَدَيْهِ،
فَيَرُدَّهُمَا صِفْرًا أَوْ قَالَ: خَائِبَتَيْنِ

Verily your Lord is the One modest and generous, and when His servant raises his hands to Him in supplication, He is shy in returning them empty.

(Sunan Ibn Mājah, Vol. 2, Pg. 1271)

In another narration, it is reported:

وَيَسْتَحْيِي أَنْ يُعَذِّبَ شَيْبَةً شَابَتْ فِي الْإِسْلَامِ

Allāh is shy to punish a person who has grown old on Islām (i.e. Has white hair)

We realise that modesty and shyness are attributes which are associated with Allāh ﷻ also. This gives us an indication of how important and praiseworthy this quality is.

Modesty: Quality Passed Down By Prophets

There are some qualities which are passed down from generation to generation over the centuries. One of these qualities is modesty, which has been passed down from the earliest Prophets and has reached us.

Ḥaḍrat Abū Mas'ūd 'Uqbah narrates that the Prophet said:

إِنَّ مِمَّا أَدْرَكَ النَّاسُ مِنْ كَلَامِ النُّبُوَّةِ، إِذَا لَمْ تَسْتَحِيْ فَافْعَلْ مَا شِئْتَ

Among the things that people have found from the words of the previous Prophets was: 'If you feel no shame, then do as you wish.'

(Ṣaḥīḥ al-Bukhārī, Vol. 4, Pg. 177)

Many of the practices of the nations of the previous Prophets were cancelled and terminated by Islām; modesty is one of the few things which Islām kept. The words of the Ḥadīth are the same as a term which is still used to this day. It is said, "Bey Ḥayā Bāsh, Har Che Khwāhi Kun" which means, 'Once a person become shameless, he does not care what anyone thinks about any act that he carries out.' He does not worry what people will say or think, rather he ignores them and does whatever he wants.

Modesty Emphasised in the Qur'ān

The importance and necessity of modesty can also be seen from the fact that it is mentioned in numerous verses of the Holy Qur'ān, where it is described as a praiseworthy trait. We shall mention some of those verses.

Modesty is One of the Qualities of a Believer

One of the most important qualities mentioned by the Qur'ān of those who will attain success is that they protect and guard their private parts. The Holy Qur'ān states:

وَالَّذِيْنَ هُمْ لِفُرُوْجِهِمْ حٰفِظُوْنَ ۞ اِلَّا عَلٰى اَزْوَاجِهِمْ اَوْ مَا مَلَكَتْ اَيْمَانُهُمْ فَاِنَّهُمْ غَيْرُ مَلُوْمِيْنَ ۞ فَمَنِ ابْتَغٰى وَرَآءَ ذٰلِكَ فَاُولٰٓئِكَ هُمُ الْعٰدُوْنَ ۞

And who guard their private organs. Except from their wives or the legal bondwomen that they possess, for then there is no blame upon them. So whoever desires more than these two – they are crossing the limits.

(Sūrah al-Mu'minūn, Chapter 23, Verses 5-7)

Success Lies in Modesty and Chastity

In mentioning the order for modesty and covering one's self, Allāh ﷻ states:

قُلْ لِّلْمُؤْمِنِيْنَ يَغُضُّوْا مِنْ اَبْصَارِهِمْ وَيَحْفَظُوْا فُرُوْجَهُمْ ۚ ذٰلِكَ اَزْكٰى لَهُمْ ۚ اِنَّ اللهَ خَبِيْرٌ بِمَا يَصْنَعُوْنَ ۞ وَقُلْ لِّلْمُؤْمِنٰتِ يَغْضُضْنَ مِنْ اَبْصَارِهِنَّ وَيَحْفَظْنَ فُرُوْجَهُنَّ وَلَا يُبْدِيْنَ زِيْنَتَهُنَّ اِلَّا مَا ظَهَرَ مِنْهَا وَلْيَضْرِبْنَ بِخُمُرِهِنَّ عَلٰى جُيُوْبِهِنَّ ۠ وَلَا يُبْدِيْنَ زِيْنَتَهُنَّ اِلَّا لِبُعُوْلَتِهِنَّ اَوْ اٰبَآئِهِنَّ اَوْ اٰبَآءِ بُعُوْلَتِهِنَّ اَوْ اَبْنَآئِهِنَّ اَوْ اَبْنَآءِ بُعُوْلَتِهِنَّ اَوْ اِخْوَانِهِنَّ اَوْ بَنِيْٓ اِخْوَانِهِنَّ اَوْ بَنِيْٓ اَخَوَاتِهِنَّ اَوْ نِسَآئِهِنَّ اَوْ مَا مَلَكَتْ اَيْمَانُهُنَّ اَوِ التّٰبِعِيْنَ غَيْرِ اُولِى الْاِرْبَةِ مِنَ الرِّجَالِ اَوِ الطِّفْلِ الَّذِيْنَ لَمْ يَظْهَرُوْا عَلٰى عَوْرٰتِ النِّسَآءِ ۠ وَلَا يَضْرِبْنَ بِاَرْجُلِهِنَّ لِيُعْلَمَ مَا يُخْفِيْنَ مِنْ زِيْنَتِهِنَّ ۚ وَتُوْبُوْٓا اِلَى اللهِ جَمِيْعًا اَيُّهَ الْمُؤْمِنُوْنَ لَعَلَّكُمْ تُفْلِحُوْنَ

Command the Muslim men to keep their gaze low and to protect their private organs; that is much purer for them; indeed Allāh is aware of their deeds. And command the Muslim women to keep their gaze low and to protect their chastity, and not to reveal their adornment except what is apparent, and to keep the cover wrapped over their bosoms; and not to reveal their adornment except to their own husbands or fathers or husbands' fathers, or their sons or their husbands' sons, or their brothers or their brothers' sons or sisters' sons, or women of their religion, or the bondwomen they possess, or male servants provided they do not have manliness, or such children who do not know of women's nakedness, and not to stamp their feet on the ground in order that their hidden adornment be known; and O Muslims, all of you turn in repentance together towards Allāh, in the hope of attaining success.

(Sūrah al-Nūr, 24: 30-31)

We are told in this verse that it is incumbent for men to keep their gaze lowered and for women to cover themselves properly. It is stated that some of the blessed wives were with the Prophet ﷺ when Ḥaḍrat 'Abdullāh ibn Umme Maktūm ؓ came by. The Prophet ﷺ ordered the blessed wives to cover themselves (appropriately). They said, "But he is blind." The Prophet ﷺ replied, "But you are not blind." (Tirmidhī, Abū Dāwūd)

From this Ḥadīth, we learn that it is also impermissible for females to look at and be in the presence of a *ghayr maḥram*.* From the verse of the Qur'ān, it is also ordered that women must not stamp their feet or walk in such a manner in their homes that their jewellery can be heard. This is why women should not wear anklets with bells on them. It is stated in Ḥadīth that Allāh ﷻ does not accept the supplication of the community whose women wear anklets with bells on them. We should realise from this that when the sound of jewellery becomes the reason for supplications not being accepted, how much wrath would the actual voice of a woman (communicating with a *ghayr maḥram* male) and her being uncovered incur? May Allāh protect. (Tafsīr Aḥmadī etc.)

* **NOTE:** *A Maḥram refers to any relative whom a person is not allowed to marry. In other words, one who is forbidden permanently to marry (i.e. father, brother, son, mother, sister, daughter etc.) A Ghayr Maḥram refers to all others with whom marriage is permissible. For ease of*

understanding, the words Maḥram and Ghayr Maḥram will be used from this point forward.

Promise of a Great Reward for the Modest

Modest people are promised forgiveness and a great reward. Allāh ﷻ states:

وَالْحٰفِظِيْنَ فُرُوْجَهُمْ وَالْحٰفِظٰتِ وَالذّٰكِرِيْنَ اللّٰهَ كَثِيْرًا وَّالذّٰكِرٰتِ اَعَدَّ اللّٰهُ لَهُمْ
مَّغْفِرَةً وَّاَجْرًا عَظِيْمًا

... and the men who guard their chastity and the women who guard their chastity, and the men who profusely remember Allāh and the women who profusely remember Allāh – for all of them, Allāh has kept prepared forgiveness and an immense reward.

(Sūrah al-Aḥzāb, 33: 35)

In this verse, the qualities which guarantee a person forgiveness and a great reward include modesty and chastity.

Daughters of Ḥaḍrat Shu'aib عليه السلام Mentioned in the Qur'ān

The Holy Qur'ān points towards a beautiful incident regarding modesty which teaches a valuable lesson to Muslim women about how they should leave their homes.

Ḥaḍrat Mūsā عليه السلام is a great Prophet with whom Allāh ﷻ communicated directly, which is why he is known as *'Kalīmullāh'* (one who talked to Allāh). One time, he was on a journey and it was very hot. He was walking bare-footed. Due to the heat and the long journey, his feet had become blistered. He sat under the shade of a tree in order to get some rest. He saw a well in the distance where some youngsters were drawing water and giving it to their goats to drink. He also saw two modest females standing a short distance away from these youngsters. Upon seeing them, he was shocked as to why these two girls were standing in the wilderness and who they were waiting for. When Sayyidunā Mūsā عليه السلام enquired, he learnt that these two ladies did not have a brother and their father was quite old and not capable of getting around. They had come to get water for their goats and were waiting for the rest to leave before they would draw water and give it to their goats.

After hearing this, Ḥaḍrat Mūsā عليه السلام himself went and drew water from the well and gave it to their goats. When the girls returned home earlier than usual, their father asked them why this was the case. They both relayed the whole incident to their father. Their father himself was also a Prophet and told them to go and call the young man so he could repay him for his kindness. When one of the sisters went to call Sayyidunā Mūsā عليه السلام, how did she go? What was her manner? The Qur'ān describes her approach, which was overflowing with modesty and shyness, in the following manner:

فَجَآءَتْهُ اِحْدٰىهُمَا تَمْشِیْ عَلَى اسْتِحْيَآءٍ قَالَتْ اِنَّ اَبِیْ يَدْعُوْكَ
لِيَجْزِيَكَ اَجْرَ مَا سَقَيْتَ لَنَا فَلَمَّا جَآءَهٗ وَقَصَّ عَلَيْهِ الْقَصَصَ
قَالَ لَا تَخَفْ نَجَوْتَ مِنَ الْقَوْمِ الظّٰلِمِيْنَ

So one of the two women approached him, walking shyly; she said, "My father is calling you, in order to give you wages because you watered our animals for us"; when Mūsā came to him and had told him the story, he said, "Do not fear, you are safe from the unjust people."

(Sūrah al-Qaṣaṣ, 28: 25)

The daughter of Ḥaḍrat Shu'aib عليه السلام had come to call Ḥaḍrat Mūsā عليه السلام. However, she did not forsake her modesty, her gaze was lowered and she also spoke very shyly. Allāh ﷻ liked this act of hers so much that He made it a part of the Qur'ān and revealed it to His Beloved Prophet ﷺ. This was to teach all the women of the Ummah that when you leave your homes, do not forsake modesty. Rather, when you walk, walk with the gaze lowered and in such a manner that modesty becomes clearly evident in your walk and your speech; just as the daughter of Ḥaḍrat Shu'aib عليه السلام had walked.

Merits of Modesty Emphasised in Aḥādīth

From the evil practices which were prevalent during the days of ignorance, two of these evil practices were immodesty and shamelessness. In those days, women would go out and walk arrogantly with a strut and would display their beauty and glamour for men to look at. They would wear clothes which would not cover their bodies. This has been mentioned in the Qur'ān:

وَقَرْنَ فِي بُيُوتِكُنَّ وَلَا تَبَرَّجْنَ تَبَرُّجَ الْجَاهِلِيَّةِ الْأُولَىٰ

And remain in your houses and do not unveil yourselves like the unveiling prevalent in the times of ignorance.

(Sūrah al-Aḥzāb, 33: 33)

With the advent of Islām, just as other evil practices were outlawed, clear orders were given in order to rid society of immodesty and shamelessness. The whole life of the Prophet ﷺ is an unmatched and shining example of modesty, purity and chastity. Modesty has been emphasised time and again in the blessed Aḥādīth. The merits and excellences of those who are modest have also been mentioned in many places.

Leader of the Modest People

In terms of the matchless modesty of the Prophet ﷺ, Sayyidunā Abū Sa'īd al-Khudrī ؓ reports:

كَانَ رَسُولُ اللهِ صَلَّى اللهُ عَلَيْهِ وَسَلَّمَ أَشَدَّ حَيَاءً مِنْ عَذْرَاءَ فِي خِدْرِهَا،

وَكَانَ إِذَا كَرِهَ شَيْئًا رُئِيَ ذٰلِكَ فِي وَجْهِهِ

The Prophet of Allāh ﷺ was more bashful (modest) than a virgin concealed in her veil. Whenever he would dislike something it would be perceived from his face.

(Sunan Ibn Mājah, Vol. 2, Pg. 1399)

The level of modesty of the Prophet ﷺ is very evident from the Ḥadīth mentioned above. If he ﷺ was displeased with or disliked something, out of modesty he would not say anything. However, the displeasure could be seen on his blessed face. In testifying to the chastity and purity of the Prophet ﷺ, Sayyidah 'Āisha Ṣiddīqa states:

مَا لَمَسَتْ يَدُهُ يَدَ امْرَاءَةٍ قَطُّ لَا يَمْلِكُ رِقَّهَا

He (the Prophet ﷺ) never touched the hand of any woman who was not his wife.

(Al-Shifā bi Ta'rīf al-Ĥuqūq al-Muṣṭafā, Vol. 1, Pg. 271)

Modesty is a Characteristic of Islām

Sayyidunā Anas ibn Mālik رضي الله عنه narrates that the Prophet ﷺ said:

اِنَّ لِكُلِّ دِينٍ خُلُقًا وَخُلُقُ الْاِسْلَامِ الْحَيَاءُ

Every religion has a distinctive quality, and the distinctive quality of Islām is modesty.

(Sunan Ibn Mājah, Vol. 2, Pg. 1399)

This is why it has been declared to be a part of faith because faith cannot be complete without it. One of the most important distinctive qualities of Islām is modesty and it has been stated that a distinctive sign of Muslims is that they are modest. From this Ḥadīth, it becomes quite evident how important it is and how hard we should strive in order to adopt this quality. Additionally, it indicates how essential it is for us to always be modest and avoid indecency and shamelessness at all times.

Modesty Takes a Person into Paradise

It is reported by Amīr al-Mu'minīn, Ḥaḍrat Sayyidunā Abū Bakr al-Ṣiddīq رضي الله عنه that the Prophet ﷺ said:

اَلْحَيَاءُ مِنَ الْاِيمَانِ وَالْاِيمَانُ فِي الْجَنَّةِ وَالْبَذَاءُ مِنَ الْجَفَاءِ وَالْجَفَاءُ فِي النَّارِ

Modesty is part of faith and faith is in Paradise. Shamelessness is part of impudence and impudence is in the Hellfire.

(Sunan Ibn Mājah, Vol. 2, Pg. 1400)

Every person has a desire for Paradise and constantly dreams of attaining the favours and blessings which will be given in Paradise. In order to enter Paradise, it is necessary for us to adopt the qualities and characteristics of the people of Paradise. According to the Ḥadīth, one of the qualities of the people of Paradise is that they are modest. Therefore, those who desire Paradise should make it their habit to always remain modest.

Modesty Beautifies a Person

Sayyidunā Anas ﷺ narrates that the Prophet ﷺ said:

مَا كَانَ الْفُحْشُ فِي شَيْءٍ قَطُّ إِلَّا شَانَهُ، وَلَا كَانَ الْحَيَاءُ فِي شَيْءٍ قَطُّ إِلَّا زَانَهُ

Respect is lost for anything which contains immodesty and the beauty of anything which contains modesty is increased.

(Sunan Ibn Mājah, Vol. 2, Pg. 1400)

This narration makes it very clear that the beauty of humans lies in modesty and one who possesses this quality will be beautified even more. The opposite of this is that the person who is immodest and shameless will definitely lose honour and respect.

Paradise Guaranteed for the Chaste

The importance, significance and merits of modesty are also highlighted in the narrations in which the Prophet ﷺ has guaranteed Paradise in exchange for modesty. Ḥaḍrat Sahal bin S'ad ﷺ narrates that the Prophet ﷺ said:

مَنْ يَضْمَنْ لِي مَا بَيْنَ لَحْيَيْهِ وَمَا بَيْنَ رِجْلَيْهِ أَضْمَنْ لَهُ الْجَنَّةَ

Whoever gives me a guarantee to safeguard what is between his legs (his private parts) and what is between his jaws (his tongue), I shall guarantee him Paradise.

(Ṣaḥīḥ al-Bukhārī, Vol. 8, Pg. 100)

Due to the fact that there is increased risk of youngsters not being able to guard their chastity, the Prophet ﷺ addressed them directly and stated:

يَا مَعْشَرَ شَبَابِ قُرَيْشٍ اِحْفَظُوا فُرُوجَكُمْ اَلَا مَنْ حَفِظَ فَرْجَهٗ فَلَهُ الْجَنَّةُ

O youngsters of Quraish! Know that whoever safeguards his private parts will be in Paradise.

(Al-Mu'jam al-Ausat lil-Ṭabarānī, Vol. 7, Pg. 61)

Both of the above Aḥādīth make it quite clear that modesty will undoubtedly lead a person into Paradise, because safeguarding the private parts will also safeguard a person from a number of other evils.

Words of Pious Predecessors Regarding Modesty

In order to further understand the importance of modesty, let us look at the words of some of the pious predecessors of this Ummah. We shall present the words of a few of them. Read them carefully and safeguard them in your hearts and minds.

Sayyidunā Abū Bakr al-Ṣiddīq ☙

Whilst delivering a sermon, Sayyidunā Abū Bakr ☙ said:

يَا مَعْشَرَ الْمُسْلِمِينَ اسْتَحْيُوا مِنَ اللهِ فَوَالَّذِي نَفْسِي بِيَدِهِ إِنِّي لَأَظَلُّ حِينَ
أَذْهَبُ إِلَى الْغَائِطِ فِي الْفَضَاءِ مُتَقَنِّعًا بِثَوْبِي اسْتِحْيَاءً مِنْ رَبِّي عَزَّ وَجَلَّ

O Muslims! Be shy in front of Allāh. By Him in Whose control is my life, when I go to a low-lying area and sit to answer the call of nature, I wrap my clothes around me because I am shy in front of Allāh ﷻ.

(Al-Zuhad wa al-Raqāiq li Ibn al-Mubārak, Vol. 1, Pg. 107)

Two things are worth noting in this narration. The first is that Sayyidunā Abū Bakr al-Ṣiddīq ☙ emphasised the need to be shy in front of Allāh ﷻ. The second is that he explained how he himself acts on that order by wrapping himself completely in his clothes when answering the call of nature. That way, there is no possibility of anyone seeing his private parts.

Sayyidunā 'Umar al-Fārūq ☙

Ḥaḍrat Aḥnaf bin al-Qais ☙ reports that Sayyidunā 'Umar ☙ gave him advice on a number of matters. He states that in relation to modesty, the Commander of the Faithful said:

مَنْ كَثُرَ كَلَامُهُ كَثُرَ سَقَطُهُ وَمَنْ كَثُرَ سَقَطُهُ قَلَّ حَيَاؤُهُ وَمَنْ قَلَّ حَيَاؤُهُ
قَلَّ وَرَعُهُ وَمَنْ قَلَّ وَرَعُهُ مَاتَ قَلْبُهُ

The one who talks more is disgraced more; the one who is disgraced more has less modesty; the one who has less modesty is less pious; and the one who has less piety has a heart which is dead.

(Al-Mu'jam al-Ausat lil-Ṭabarānī, Vol. 2, Pg. 370)

Sayyidunā 'Umar ﷺ has explained quite eloquently and beautifully that a person who is disgraced shall have less modesty. The more they are disgraced, the less modesty they shall have. This shows that modesty is a sign that a person is respectful and respected. The more respected a person is, the more modesty he shall have.

Ḥaḍrat 'Umar bin 'Abd al-'Azīz ﷺ

Ḥaḍrat Ayās bin al-Qurrah ﷺ said:

كُنَّا عِنْدَ عُمَرَ بْنِ عَبْدِ الْعَزِيزِ فَذُكِرَ عِنْدَهُ الْحَيَاءُ فَقَالَ: الْحَيَاءُ مِنَ الْإِيمَانِ فَقَالَ عُمَرُ: بَلْ هُوَ الدِّينُ كُلُّهُ

We were with Ḥaḍrat 'Umar bin 'Abd al-'Azīz ﷺ and the conversation turned to modesty. Someone said, "Modesty is a part of faith." Ḥaḍrat 'Umar bin 'Abd al-'Azīz ﷺ said, "No! Rather, it is complete faith."

(Shu'ab al-Īmān lil-Baihaqī, Vol. 10, Pg. 151)

The basis for the above statement of Ḥaḍrat 'Umar bin 'Abd al-'Azīz ﷺ is the following Ḥadīth of the Prophet ﷺ. After hearing the words of Ḥaḍrat 'Umar bin 'Abd al-'Azīz ﷺ, Ḥaḍrat Ayās ﷺ said:

كُنَّا عِنْدَ النَّبِيِّ صَلَّى اللهُ عَلَيْهِ وَسَلَّمَ فَذُكِرَ عِنْدَهُ الْحَيَاءُ فَقَالُوا: يَا رَسُولَ اللهِ الْحَيَاءُ مِنَ الدِّينِ؟ فَقَالَ النَّبِيُّ صَلَّى اللهُ عَلَيْهِ وَسَلَّمَ: بَلْ هُوَ الدِّينُ كُلُّهُ۔ ثُمَّ قَالَ رَسُولُ اللهِ صَلَّى اللهُ عَلَيْهِ وَسَلَّمَ: إِنَّ الْحَيَاءَ وَالْعَفَافَ وَالْعِيَّ عَنِ اللِّسَانِ لَا عَنِ الْقَلْبِ وَالْعَمَلِ مِنَ الْإِيمَانِ، وَإِنَّهُنَّ يُزِدْنَ فِي الْآخِرَةِ وَيُنْقِصْنَ مِنَ الدُّنْيَا وَمَا يُزِدْنَ فِي الْآخِرَةِ أَكْثَرُ مِمَّا يُنْقِصْنَ مِنَ الدُّنْيَا وَإِنَّ الشُّحَّ وَالْفُحْشَ وَالْبَذَاءَ مِنَ النِّفَاقِ وَإِنَّهُنَّ يَزِدْنَ فِي الدُّنْيَا وَيُنْقِصْنَ مِنَ الْآخِرَةِ، وَمَا يُنْقِصْنَ مِنَ الْآخِرَةِ أَكْثَرُ مِمَّا يَزِدْنَ فِي الدُّنْيَا

We were with the Prophet ﷺ and the subject of modesty was brought up. The Prophet ﷺ was asked, "O Prophet of Allāh ﷺ! Is modesty a part of faith?" The Prophet ﷺ replied, "No! Rather, it is complete faith." He then added, "Modesty, chastity and humilitythrough actions, not merely with the heart, is a part of faith. These things increase (a person in rank) in the hereafter and decrease him (in rank) in this world. However, the increase (in rank that these things give

him) in the hereafter is much more than the decreased (rank) in this world. Miserliness, indecent talk, and shamelessness is a part of hypocrisy. These things increase a person in this world and decrease him in the hereafter. However, the decreased (rank) in the hereafter is much greater than the increased (rank) in this world."

(Ibid)

In this narration, the Prophet ﷺ has explained the importance of modesty and the evils of shamelessness in detail. The benefit of modesty and the damaging effects of immodesty are not limited to just this world, rather, they are carried over into the hereafter. Modesty and chastity will lead to increased rewards in the hereafter, with increased rank and abundant favours and bounties. Even if modesty and chastity decreases a person's respect or status in this world, Allāh ﷻ increases that person's respect because of it. If Allāh ﷻ grants a person respect, who can disgrace and humiliate such a person?

Ḥaḍrat Wahab bin Munabbih ﷺ

Ḥaḍrat 'Abd al-'Azīz bin Rūfī' al-Asadī ﷺ reports that Ḥaḍrat Wahab bin Munabbih ﷺ said:

اَلْإِيمَانُ عُرْيَانٌ وَلِبَاسُهُ التَّقْوٰى وَمَالُهُ الْفِقْهُ وَزِيْنَتُهُ الْحَيَاءُ

Faith is naked and its clothing is piety, its wealth is jurisprudence and its beauty is modesty.

(Muṣannaf Ibn Abī Shaibah, Vol. 7, Pg. 191)

This shows us that without modesty, faith is incomplete. If a person has belief and also has modesty, then this is 'icing on the cake.' In the same manner, faith is incomplete without piety and jurisprudence (religious knowledge) is considered the wealth of faith. All of these together completes one's faith.

Root of Noble Character is Modesty

Sayyidunā Abū Hurairah narrates that the Prophet said:

إِنَّمَا بُعِثْتُ لِأُتَمِّمَ مَكَارِمَ الْأَخْلَاقِ

Verily I have been sent to perfect good moral character.

(Sunan al-Kubrā, Vol. 10, Pg. 323)

What is this 'good moral character'? In explaining this, Ḥaḍrat Sayyidah 'Āisha Ṣiddīqa stated:

كَانَ نَبِيُّ اللهِ صَلَّى اللهُ عَلَيْهِ وَسَلَّمَ يَقُولُ فِي مَكَارِمِ الْأَخْلَاقِ: عَشَرَةٌ تَكُونُ فِي الرَّجُلِ وَلَا تَكُونُ فِي ابْنِهٖ وَتَكُونُ فِي الْاِبْنِ وَلَا تَكُونُ فِي أَبِيهِ وَتَكُونُ فِي الْعَبْدِ وَلَا تَكُونُ فِي سَيِّدِهٖ يَقْسِمُهَا اللهُ لِمَنْ أَرَادَ بِهِ السَّعَادَةَ: صِدْقُ الْحَدِيثِ وَصِدْقُ النَّاسِ وَهُوَ أَنْ لَا يَشْبَعَ وَجَارُهٗ وَصَاحِبُهٗ جَائِعَانِ وَإِعْطَاءُ السَّائِلِ وَالْمُكَافَأَةُ بِالصَّنَائِعِ وَحِفْظُ الْأَمَانَةِ وَصِلَةُ الرَّحِمِ وَالتَّذَمُّمُ لِلْجَارِ وَالتَّذَمُّمُ لِلصَّاحِبِ وَإِقْرَاءُ الضَّيْفِ وَرَأْسُهُنَّ الْحَيَاءُ

In relation to good moral character, the Prophet would say, "It is ten qualities. A father may have them but his children may not. A child may have them but his father may not. A slave may have them but his master may not. Whomever Allāh desires goodness for, He grants them these qualities. (1) Truth in speech (2) Sympathy, meaning if your neighbour or friend is hungry, you are not able to eat (3) Giving to beggars (4) Moderation in all things (5) Safeguarding trusts (6) Kindness towards relatives (7) Humility with neighbours (8) Humility with friends (9) Hospitality (10) The root of good moral character is modesty.

(Shu'ab al-Īmān lil-Baihaqī, Vol. 10, Pg. 161)

We realise that the Prophet came into the world to perfect our moral character. One of the most important morals which he came to perfect is modesty. This quality was present in the beloved Prophet himself and he invited all of humanity to adopt this quality too.

Types and Reasons for Modesty

There are two basic forms of modesty – 1) natural and 2) acquired. Natural modesty is the modesty which is inherently present in a person; what they were born with. Some people have a lot of it and some people have a little. Acquired modesty is dependent on a person. They can choose to increase or decrease it as they wish. As far as reasons are concerned, there are ten types. This is because there are ten reasons why a person would feel modest or feel shame in front of another.

First Reason: Crime or Sin

A person is filled with shame if he commits a mistake. In Arabic, this is referred to as 'حَيَاءُ الْجِنَايَة' (Ḥayā ul-Jināyah). It is reported that when Sayyidunā Ādam عليه السلام made a mistake in judgement (*Khatā-e-Ijtihādī*) and ate from the tree which was forbidden, his clothing was removed. Then, when he began to run away, Allāh عزوجل said, 'أَفِرَارًا مِنِّيْ يَا آدَمُ؟' (O Ādam! Are you running away from Me?) Sayyidunā Ādam عليه السلام said, 'لَا يَا رَبِّ بَلْ حَيَاءً مِنْكَ' (No my Lord! Rather, I am shy in front of You).

It is stated in Tafsīr al-Khāzin:
'After coming onto the earth, Sayyidunā Ādam عليه السلام did not raise his head towards the heavens for 300 years due to shame and modesty. Sayyidunā Dāwūd عليه السلام is known as one who wept constantly and his tears are greater (in number) than the tears of all who are on the earth. However, Ḥaḍrat Ādam عليه السلام cried so much that his tears were more than the tears of Sayyidunā Dāwūd عليه السلام and the people on the earth combined.'

Second Reason: Underperforming

This is also a reason for feeling ashamed. If a person is given a specific task to complete and he is not able to complete it, for whatever reason, it is natural to feel embarrassed or ashamed. It is stated in Ḥadīth that the Prophet ﷺ said:

مَا فِي السَّمٰوَاتِ السَّبْعِ مَوْضِعُ قَدَمٍ وَّلَا شِبْرٍ وَّلَا كَفٍّ اِلَّا وَفِيْهِ مَلَكٌ قَائِمٌ
اَوْ مَلَكٌ سَاجِدٌ اَوْ مَلَكٌ رَاكِعٌ فَاِذَا كَانَ يَوْمُ الْقِيَامَةِ قَالُوْا جَمِيْعًا: سُبْحَانَكَ
مَا عَبَدْنَاكَ حَقَّ عِبَادَتِكَ

There is not a single spot in the seven heavens where an Angel is not standing, bowing or prostrating (in Prayer). On the Day of Judgement, they will all say, "Praise be to You! We have not fulfilled the rights of worshipping You."

(Tafsīr Ibn Kathīr, Vol. 8, Pg. 270)

Third Reason: Respect

The more respect a person has in his heart for the Majesty and Greatness of Allāh ﷻ, the more shy and modest he will be of Him ﷻ.

Fourth Reason: Grace and Kindness

Grace and kindness can also be a reason for modesty and shyness. The Prophet ﷺ was modest in this regard also. When the Prophet ﷺ performed marriage with Ḥaḍrat Zainab رضي الله عنها and invited the people for a wedding feast (*Walīmah*), groups of people would come, eat and then leave. At the end, there were three people who had finished eating but stayed there and were busy in conversation with each other for a long period of time. The house was small and it was inconvenient for the members of the household as they were not able to complete their chores because of these guests. The Prophet ﷺ got up and went to the rooms of the blessed wives and returned after a while. The guests were still busy with their conversation. The Prophet ﷺ once again got up and left. Upon seeing this, the guests also left. After they had left, Prophet ﷺ placed a cover over the door of the home. It was after this incident that the following verse of the Qur'ān was revealed:

يٰٓاَيُّهَا الَّذِيْنَ اٰمَنُوْا لَا تَدْخُلُوْا بُيُوْتَ النَّبِيِّ اِلَّآ اَنْ يُّؤْذَنَ لَكُمْ اِلٰى طَعَامٍ غَيْرَ نٰظِرِيْنَ اِنٰىهُ ۙ
وَلٰكِنْ اِذَا دُعِيْتُمْ فَادْخُلُوْا فَاِذَا طَعِمْتُمْ فَانْتَشِرُوْا وَلَا مُسْتَاْنِسِيْنَ لِحَدِيْثٍ ؕ اِنَّ ذٰلِكُمْ
كَانَ يُؤْذِى النَّبِيَّ فَيَسْتَحْيٖ مِنْكُمْ ۫ وَاللّٰهُ لَا يَسْتَحْيٖ مِنَ الْحَقِّ

O People who Believe! Do not enter the houses of the Prophet without permission, as when called for a meal but not to linger around waiting for it; and if you are invited then certainly present yourself and when you have eaten, disperse – not staying around delighting in conversation; indeed that was causing harassment to the Prophet, and he was having regard for you; and Allāh is not shy in proclaiming the truth;

(Sūrah al-Aḥzāb, 33: 53)

This incident displays the supreme modesty, grace and kindness of the Prophet ﷺ. In spite of there being a genuine reason, added to the fact that they had eaten and fulfilled the reason that they were invited, he did not ask the Companions to leave. The manner that he ﷺ adopted was the best example of manners and etiquettes.

Fifth Reason: Commanding Personality

A person's commanding personality or awe can also be a reason for being shy or modest in their presence. Just as Sayyidunā 'Alī ؓ was shy in asking the Prophet ﷺ about seminal discharge due to the commanding personality and awe of the Prophet ﷺ. However, it was necessary to find out the answer to the question. Therefore, he asked Ḥaḍrat Miqdād ؓ to ask the question, who then asked the Prophet ﷺ and subsequently informed Sayyidunā 'Alī ؓ of the reply.

Sixth Reason: Humility

This is also a reason for feeling shy and shameful. For example, when supplicating, a person may feel embarrassed because he thinks to himself, 'I have no (good) deeds and still I am raising my hands and asking for things from such a supreme and majestic court.'

Seventh Reason: Love

Love is also a reason for feeling shyness. Just as when someone sees their beloved, they are overcome with a sense of modesty and shyness, which makes their beauty stand out even more. If a wife has this kind of shyness or modesty, a husband loves her beauty even more.

Eighth Reason: Worship

Worship is also a reason for modesty and shyness. This is a combination of shyness and fear. This is the shyness which does not allow a person to disobey the Lord.

Ninth Reason: Honour and Dignity

This is also a reason in that a person would feel shy to do something in front of another due to that person's stature, honour and dignity. Or, for example, not committing a sin because a person realises that Allāh ﷻ is watching him.

Tenth Reason: Self-Modesty

This is a great form of modesty. This trait is specifically helpful in avoiding sins when a person is alone and in private as it ensures that he does not commit sins even in private.

Two Kinds of Modesty

There are actually two kinds of modesty/shyness. One is that which does not allow a person to participate fully in acts of goodness; this is a contemptible kind of modesty. The second is one which stops a person from committing evil; this is a beloved form of modesty. Details of both kinds are as follows:

Contemptible Modesty

Many people blame shyness when refraining from carrying out acts of goodness. They feel embarrassed in inviting to good and forbidding from evil. The reality is that this is not shyness or modesty, rather it is a form of laziness which people call shyness. According to the blessed Aḥādīth, there was no one more modest and shy than the beloved Prophet ﷺ; nor will there be anybody more shy and modest until the Day of Judgement. In spite of this, he ﷺ never hesitated in inviting to good, forbidding from evil and propagating the religion and religious teachings.

In the same way, shyness cannot be a barrier in seeking knowledge and learning about the religion and religious issues and rulings. Sayyidah 'Āisha Ṣiddīqa رضي الله عنها stated:

نِعْمَ النِّسَآءُ نِسَآءُ الْاَنْصَارِ لَمْ يَكُنْ يَمْنَعُهُنَّ الْحَيَآءُ اَنْ يَّتَفَقَّهْنَ فِي الدِّيْنِ

How good are the women of the Anṣār for, in seeking religious knowledge, they do not allow shyness to be a barrier for them.

(Ṣaḥīḥ al-Bukhārī, Vol. 1, Pg. 38)

According to one narration, Sayyidah Umme Sulaim رضي الله عنها came to the Prophet ﷺ and said, "Allāh ﷻ does not shy away from the truth. If a woman has a wet dream, is bathing compulsory for her?" The Prophet ﷺ said, "Yes, if she sees fluid." Upon hearing this, Sayyidah Umme Salamah رضي الله عنها covered her face and asked, "O Prophet of Allāh ﷺ! Do women also have wet dreams?" The Prophet ﷺ replied, "Yes of course. That is why her child resembles her." (Ibid. Pg. 130)

Beloved Modesty

There are three kinds of modesty/shyness which are beloved and worthy of praise – 1) in front of Allāh ﷻ, 2) in front of the Angels, 3) in front of people.

Modesty in Front of Allāh ﷻ

Modesty in front of Allāh ﷻ is when it is firmly planted in a person's heart that Allāh ﷻ is watching, is hearing the words and every moment and every action is seen by Allāh ﷻ. A person who develops this mentality will be ashamed to be short in their obligatory worships, or to commit any sins. For example, if a man sees a woman in private and, with lustful intention, says, "There is no one to see us here except for the stars." Upon hearing this, the woman says, "Yes, but where is the One Who created the stars?"

Allāh ﷻ is Watching

It is reported that a wealthy person went into his orchard. There he saw the gardener sitting with his wife. Due to the beauty and attractiveness of the gardener's wife, the wealthy man was attracted to her. Evil thoughts and intentions entered into his heart. He sent the gardener off to run an errand. When the two of them were alone, he told the gardener's wife to close all the entrances to the orchard.

The woman immediately realised what his intentions were. When she went back to him, he asked, "Are all the doors closed?" She replied, "Yes, except for one door." He asked, "Which door is that?" She replied, "The one which is between me and my Lord." Upon hearing this, a great feeling of fear overcame the man and he burst into tears and left. (Kashf al-Maḥjūb)

Meaning of Modesty from Allāh ﷻ

True modesty and shyness is for a person to be modest in front of Allāh ﷻ. Detailed explanation of modesty from Allāh ﷻ is present in Aḥādīth. Sayyidunā 'Abdullāh ibn Mas'ūd ؓ narrates that the Prophet ﷺ climbed onto the pulpit and said:

أَيُّهَا النَّاسُ اِسْتَحْيُوْا مِنَ اللهِ حَقَّ الْحَيَاءِ

O People! Be modest in front of Allāh for He has a right to your modesty.

Someone asked:

يَا رَسُوْلَ اللهِ اِنَّا لَنَسْتَحْيِي مِنَ اللهِ

O Prophet of Allah! We are modest in front of Allāh.

The Prophet ﷺ said:

مَنْ كَانَ مِنْكُمْ مُسْتَحْيِيًا فَلَا يَبِيْتَنَّ لَيْلَةً اِلَّا وَأَجَلُهُ بَيْنَ عَيْنَيْهِ

Each night of the one who is modest in front of Allāh ﷻ should be spent in such a manner that his death is in front of him.

The words of explanation then given by the Prophet ﷺ are worthy of memorising and ingraining into our hearts and minds. He said:

وَلْيَحْفَظِ الْبَطْنَ وَمَا وَعٰى

And he should safeguard his stomach and the organs close to it.

We have been told in this narration that if a person claims to be modest in front of Allāh ﷻ, he should ensure that his stomach and the organs close to it are safeguarded. Safeguarding the stomach means to ensure that unlawful food does not enter it. The organs close to it are – 1) the private parts, 2) the arms, 3) the legs.

Safeguarding the stomach, private parts, arms and legs is a complete topic in itself. Extensive detail on them is available in our other publications. Refer to them for details.

Modesty from Allāh ﷻ – Safeguarding the Head

The Prophet ﷺ continued on and said:

وَالرَّأْسَ وَمَا حَوٰى

(And safeguard) the head and everything associated with it.

The parts associated with the head are:

1. The brain: safeguarding it means that a person's thinking and mind-set should conform with the Sharī'ah and intentions should be correct.
2. Safeguarding the eyes from viewing disallowed things and from looking at impermissible men/women.
3. Safeguarding the ears from listening to backbiting, lies, music and useless talk.
4. Safeguarding the nose from smelling the perfume of those who are impermissible.
5. Safeguarding the tongue from lies, backbiting, telling tales, songs, swearing and unlawful words.

A Common Indecency of this Era

One form of shamelessness through the hands, tongue and ears has become very common nowadays. The 'chatting' and 'texting' which occurs between young males and females on the phone is completely forbidden by Sharī'ah. This will be the means of great disgrace, humiliation and sorrow in this world and the hereafter.

Parents who, out of love and affection, give mobile phones to their children at a young age, should ensure that they keep an eye on those phones and check them regularly. If they are involved in the aforementioned evils, they will also be called to account on the Day of Judgement.

Remember Difficulties of the Grave

The Prophet ﷺ continued on and said:

وَلْيَذْكُرِ الْقُبُوْرَ وَالْبِلٰى

(And he should) remember the graves and the difficulties in them.

Remembrance of death is a concept Islām has given which can save a person from thousands of sins. This is why in Aḥādīth, death has been called the 'eliminator of (unlawful) desires.'

Forsake the Decorations of the Worldly Life

The Prophet ﷺ continued on and said:

وَلْيَتْرُكْ زِيْنَةَ الْحَيَاةِ الدُّنْيَا

(And he should) forsake the decorations of this worldly life.

(Mu'jam al-Ausat lil-Ṭabarānī, Vol. 8, Pg. 226)

When a Person Becomes Immodest

Sayyidunā 'Abdullāh bin 'Umar ﷺ narrates that the Prophet ﷺ said:

اِذَا اَبْغَضَ اللهُ عَبْدًا نَزَعَ مِنْهُ الْحَيَاءَ فَاِذَا نَزَعَ مِنْهُ الْحَيَاءَ لَمْ تَلْقَهُ اِلَّا بَغِيْضًا مُبْغِضًا اَوْ نَزَعَ اللهُ مِنْهُ الْاَمَانَةَ فَاِذَا نَزَعَ مِنْهُ الْاَمَانَةَ نَزَعَ مِنْهُ الرَّحْمَةَ فَاِذَا نَزَعَ مِنْهُ الرَّحْمَةَ نَزَعَ مِنْهُ رِبْقَةَ الْاِسْلَامِ وَاِذَا نَزَعَ مِنْهُ رِبْقَةَ الْاِسْلَامِ لَمْ تَلْقَهُ اِلَّا شَيْطَانًا مَّرِيْدًا

When Allāh hates a person, He removes modesty from them. When modesty is removed, you will find him disliked in all places. Or He will remove trustworthiness from him. When his trustworthiness is removed, he no longer receives mercy. When mercy is removed from him, the knot of Islām is untied and when the knot of Islām is untied, you will find him to be a mischievous devil.

(Shu'ab al-Īmān, Vol. 10, Pg. 165)

We see that if a person has no modesty, it means that he is hated by Allāh ﷻ. That person becomes disliked in the eyes of people and also begins to breach trust. He then loses out on the Mercy of Allāh ﷻ. His relationship with Islām is weakened and such a person becomes a tool for the devils. May Allāh ﷻ grant us the treasure of modesty and shyness and protect us from shamelessness and immodesty.

The root of modesty is that a person should be shy and modest before Allāh ﷻ, who is present everywhere with His Knowledge and Divine Power. He sees every person and is aware of the actions and deeds of all. A person who is modest before Allāh ﷻ will be safeguarded from all evils.

Modesty in Front of Angels

Every person has two Angels who are appointed to him – one on his left shoulder and one on his right shoulder. The Holy Qur'ān states:

$$وَاِنَّ عَلَيْكُمْ لَحٰفِظِيْنَ ۞ كِرَامًا كَاتِبِيْنَ ۞ يَعْلَمُوْنَ مَا تَفْعَلُوْنَ ۞$$

And indeed there are some guardians over you. The honourable recorders. Knowing all what you may do.

(Sūrah al-Infiṭār, 82:10-12)

At another point, it states:

$$مَا يَلْفِظُ مِنْ قَوْلٍ اِلَّا لَدَيْهِ رَقِيْبٌ عَتِيْدٌ$$

He does not utter a single word, without a ready recorder seated next to him.

(Sūrah al-Qāf, 50:18)

Sadr al-Afāḍil, Ḥaḍrat 'Allāma Syed Na'īmuddīn Murādabādī ﵀ writes:

'Regardless of where he is – except for when answering the call of nature or having sexual relations, for the Angels move away from a person at those times (it is not permissible for a person to talk at those times so that the Angels are not grieved by having to come close to him to write them down) – these Angels record every word of a person, including the involuntary moan during times of illness. It has also been said that they only write those things which are rewarded or those which are worthy of punishment. Imām al-Baghawī has reported a Ḥadīth which states that

when a person does a good deed, the Angel on the right shoulder writes down ten good deeds. When a person commits a sin, the Angel on the right says to the Angel on the left, "Do not write it down just yet. Wait for a little while, maybe he will repent."' (Khazāin al-Irfān)

It is therefore necessary for us to have modesty in front of these respected and esteemed Angels who record our words and deeds. We must ensure that they do not see us in any improper place, or in any improper situation.

Modesty in Front of People

In reality, this identifies the level of kindness, regard and politeness a person possesses. This modesty makes a person feel embarrassed and shy in grieving another with his hands or tongue; indulging in unpleasant talk; saying insulting or obscene words; swearing, using indecent language, backbiting and telling tales about others. In the same way, this modesty also ensures that a person's body (parts which must remain covered) do not become exposed, even by accident, and that they are covered and protected from the gaze of other people at all times.

How is Desire for Modesty Attained?

In this regard, the following words of scholars and pious predecessors are very beneficial in instilling in ourselves the passion and desire to be modest at all times.

(1) Ḥaḍrat Junaid al-Baghdādī ﷺ states, "By remembering the favours of Allāh ﷻ at all times, as well as our own deficiencies, the state that results from this is called modesty." (Shu'ab al-Īmān, Vol. 7, Pg. 148)

(2) Sayyidunā Dhū al-Nūn al-Miṣrī ﷺ says, "The thing which forces a person to display modesty is recognising the favours of Allāh ﷻ and realising our shortcomings in thanking Him ﷻ for them. That is because just as there is no limit to the Majesty and Magnificence of Allāh ﷻ, there is also no limit to how much He ﷻ should be thanked." (Ibid. Vol. 6, Pg. 147)

(3) Ḥaḍrat Muḥammad ﷺ says, "Modesty is created by first of all focusing on the favours given by your Benefactor. Then you should focus on how unjust you have been in thanking Him for those favours. When you start to focus on these two things at all times, you will be blessed with the great gift of modesty, Allāh willing." (Ibid. Vol. 7, Pg. 148)

The summary of the above is that first of all, we must always remember the unmatched favours that Allāh ﷻ showers on us constantly. We must then see if we are fulfilling the rights of those favours and how deficient we are in this regard. This (constant) reminder will automatically instil in us the feeling that we should not do anything which is displeasing to our Merciful and Beneficial Lord ﷻ; or which shows disrespect of the favours given by Him ﷻ. It is this feeling which is called modesty, which is one of the best and most important qualities of a believer.

Modesty of the Pious Slaves of Allāh ﷻ

The pious slaves of Allāh ﷻ were modest at all times and their modesty and chastity is an example for all of humanity. Due to fear of Allāh ﷻ, they refrained from all deeds which went against the Sharī'ah, against etiquettes, or against the preferred option at all times. This is why their modesty was at an extremely high level. We shall mention a few examples.

Modesty of Ḥaḍrat 'Uthmān ؓ

Ḥaḍrat Sayyidah 'Āisha Ṣiddīqa ؓ reports:

'The Prophet ﷺ was lying in the bed in my apartment with his shin uncovered. Ḥaḍrat Abū Bakr ؓ sought permission to enter. It was given to him and the Prophet ﷺ conversed in the same very state (with his shin uncovered). Then Ḥaḍrat 'Umar ؓ sought permission for entering and it was given to him and he conversed in that very state. Then Ḥaḍrat 'Uthmān ؓ sought permission to come in. The Prophet ﷺ sat upright and he set right his clothes (covered his shin). Ḥaḍrat 'Uthmān ؓ then entered and conversed. After he had left, I said, "Abū Bakr entered and you did not sit up or arrange your clothes. Then 'Umar entered and you did not sit up or arrange your clothes. Then 'Uthmān entered and you got up and set your clothes right." The Prophet ﷺ said, "Should I not show modesty to one whom even the Angels show modesty towards?"' (Al-Adab al-Mufrad, Vol. 1, Pg. 311)

In mentioning the extreme modesty of Ḥaḍrat 'Uthmān ﷺ, Ḥaḍrat Imām Ḥasan ﷺ stated, "Sometimes, Ḥaḍrat 'Uthman ﷺ would be in his home and all the doors would be closed. However, his modesty would still not allow him to remove all his clothing when bathing. He was so shy and modest that after bathing, he would not stand up straight until he had properly covered the parts of the body which must be covered." (Extracted from Al-Ḥilya by Abū Nu'aim)

Modesty of Imām Ja'far al-Ṣādiq ﷺ

One day Ḥaḍrat Imām Ja'far al-Ṣādiq ﷺ was sat with some companions and he said, "Let us all make a promise to each other that, on the Day of Judgement, whichever one of us is forgiven will intercede for the rest." They said, "O beloved grandson of the Prophet! Why would you need our intercession when your grandfather is the intercessor for all of creation?" He replied, "You are right. But because of my deeds, I am ashamed to stand before my blessed grandfather." (Tadhkirah al-Auliyā, Pg. 16)

Modesty of Ḥaḍrat Abū Mūsā ﷺ

Ḥaḍrat Qatādah ﷺ reports that even when Ḥaḍrat Abū Mūsā ﷺ would bathe in a small dark room, after he had completed bathing, he would not stand up straight. Rather, he would walk whilst bending over and would wear his clothes. After he was fully clothed, then he would stand up straight. (From Abū Nu'aim)

Ḥaḍrat Anas ﷺ reports that even when Ḥaḍrat Abū Mūsā ﷺ would sleep, he would keep all his clothes on, out of fear that his private parts would become uncovered whilst he was sleeping. (Ibid)

Ḥaḍrat 'Ubādah bin Nusay ﷺ reports that when Ḥaḍrat Abū Mūsā ﷺ saw some people standing in water who were not wearing full clothing on the lower parts of their bodies, he said, "It is more preferred to me to die, be brought back to life, then die and be brought back to life, then die again and be brought back to life rather than do as these people are doing." (Abū Nu'aim)

Modesty of Haḍrat Suleymān bin Yasār ﷺ

One time, Haḍrat Suleymān bin Yasār ﷺ was travelling for pilgrimage and camped at a place. His companions went into the city for something and he was alone in his tent. Suddenly, a beautiful woman came into his tent and indicated that she wanted something. He went to give her some food but she said angrily, "I want from you the thing that women want from men. You are young, I am beautiful and this is a great opportunity for us to seek pleasure from each other." When he heard this, Haḍrat Suleymān bin Yasār ﷺ realised that shaiṭān had sent this woman to ruin his lifelong worship. He started crying profusely out of fear of Allāh ﷻ. He cried so much that the woman became embarrassed and left. Haḍrat Suleymān bin Yasār ﷺ thanked Allāh ﷻ for protecting him from sinning. When he slept that night, he saw Sayyidunā Yusuf ﷺ in his dream, who said, "Congratulations! As a friend of Allāh ﷻ, you have done the same thing which a Prophet did." (Ḥilyat al-Awliyā wa Tabqāt al-Aşfiyā, Vol. 2, Pg. 190)

Modesty of Haḍrat Junaid al-Baghdādī ﷺ

During the time of Haḍrat Junaid al-Baghdādī ﷺ, there lived a rich man with a very beautiful wife who was very proud of her beauty. One time she said to her husband, "There is no person who would see me and not desire me." Her husband said, "I expect that Haḍrat Junaid al-Baghdādī ﷺ would not care about you." The wife asked for permission to test Haḍrat Junaid al-Baghdādī ﷺ and the husband gave her permission.

The woman adorned herself and went to Haḍrat Junaid al-Baghdādī ﷺ and, under the pretence of wanting to ask a question, she removed the veil from her face. When Haḍrat Junaid al-Baghdādī's ﷺ gaze fell on the woman's face, he began chanting the Name of Allāh ﷻ loudly. This Name ingrained itself on the heart of the woman and her state changed completely. She returned home and she gave up all her pride and excessiveness. She would recite the Qur'ān all day and would spend all night on the prayer mat. Fear and awe of Allāh ﷻ ensured that tears flowed from her eyes constantly. Her husband would often say, "What did I do to Junaid al-Baghdādī that he turned my wife into a nun and made her of no use to me?"

Modesty of Ḥaḍrat Miskī رحمه الله

In the famous Iraqi city of Basra, there lived a pious person by the name of Ḥaḍrat Miskī رحمه الله. Miskī is an Arabic word which means 'one with perfume' or 'one who is perfumed'. It is reported that the only reason he became known as Miskī was because he would always give off a very pleasant smell. Even the paths which he walked on became fragranced. When he would go to the Masjid, people would realise from the pleasant fragrance that he had arrived.

Once, a person said to him, "Ḥaḍrat! You must spend quite a lot of money on perfumes and fragrances." He smiled and said, "No! I have never purchased any nor have I ever fragranced myself with 'itr or anything else. There is an amazing story behind the fact that my body gives off a beautiful fragrance." Upon being asked for details, he said, "I was born into a respectable family in Baghdad and I was educated along with children my own age. I was very beautiful and extremely shy and modest. Upon seeing the level of my shyness, someone suggested to my mother that she should make me work in the markets in order to reduce the amount of shyness and modesty I had, in order for it to be easier for me to be comfortable around people. Therefore, my mother got me a job at a shop selling cloth. One day, an old lady asked to look at a number of expensive clothes. She then said to the shopkeeper, "Send someone with me. I will try these on at home, keep the ones I like and send the rest back. I will then pay for what I keep." Therefore, the shopkeeper sent me with her.

The old lady took me to a great palace and sent me into an adjoining room. In this room, there was a young lady, dressed in expensive clothing and jewellery, sitting on a throne. This room was decorated so beautifully that I had never seen anything like that before. As soon as she saw me, shaiṭān overcame this young lady. She came close to me and began to harass me and invited me to commit a sin with her. I panicked and said, "Fear Allāh!" However, shaiṭān had total control over her and she would not stop. When I saw how persistent she was, I suddenly thought of a way in which I could avoid sinning. I said to her, "I need to go to the bathroom." She called out and dozens of servants came running. She said to them, "Show this young man the way to the bathroom." When I reached the bathroom, I saw that there was no other escape route from the bathroom and I was ashamed and embarrassed to commit a sin with the young lady in front of my Lord. I could only see one way out and therefore I took the faeces from the bathroom and spread it on my hands, face and body. I started screaming like a madman and frightened the servants so much that they started screaming also. The servants got together and wrapped me in a large blanket and threw me out into the garden. When I was sure that they had all gone, I unwrapped myself and went and cleaned my body and clothes. I then returned quietly to my home and never told anyone about this incident. That very night, I saw a pious person in my dream who asked me, "Do you recognise me?" I replied that I did not. He said, "I am Jibrīl." He then rubbed his hands on my face and body and from that time, my body gives off this beautiful fragranced smell. This is the fragrance of the hands of Jibrīl عليه السلام ." (Tafsīr Rūĥ al-Bayān, Vol. 2, Pg. 160)

A Modest Young Man

Ḥaḍrat Sayyidunā Aḥmad bin Sa'īd رحمة الله عليه reports from his father, who said:

There lived a very devout, pious and handsome young man in Kūfā, who spent most of his time in the Masjid in the remembrance of Allāh عزوجل. One time, a very beautiful and intelligent lady saw him and immediately fell in love with him. She was besotted with him and spent all her time thinking about him. When her love for him reached an unbearable stage, she went and stood on the street. A short time later, she saw the young man on his way to the Masjid. She ran to him and said, "O young man! I want to tell you something. Listen to what I have to say then do as you please." When the shy and modest young man heard the voice of this lady, he did not focus on her at all. Rather, with a lowered gaze, he continued on to the Masjid. When he was returning home from the Masjid, the lady was still there. She said, "O young man! I want to tell you something. Listen to what I have to say." With his gaze still lowered, the young man said, "This is a place where accusations are made. I do not want to be the cause of someone sinning by wrongly accusing me of something." The lady said, "By Allāh! I know your situation very well; however, I am helpless against my desires, which is why I have come here. I realise that even this kind of a meeting is considered very big in the eyes of people. Pious, sincere and pure people like yourself are like mirrors; even a small speck of dust makes it faulty. But what can I do? I am helpless in this regard. The situation of my heart is such that I spend every moment thinking of you and every part of my body is focused on you." Upon hearing this, without saying anything, the young man turned around and went home. When he got home, he wanted to pray Ṣalāh but he could not instil in himself the humility and fear of Allāh ﷻ. Finally, he wrote a letter and came outside to see that the lady was still standing there. The young man threw the letter towards her. The lady anxiously picked up the letter and started to read it. It said:

بِسْمِ اللّٰهِ الرَّحْمٰنِ الرَّحِيْمِ

O Lady! You should realise that when a person disobeys Allāh ﷻ, He forgives them. If he commits a sin again, He covers his faults. However, when a person becomes so disobedient that he continuously sins, He becomes extremely angry with him. Neither the earth, heavens, mountains, animals, humans or birds are able to withstand the anger and wrath of Allāh ﷻ. Who then has the strength to come face to face with His anger? O lady! If you are lying about what you say, then I remind you of that day When the heavens will melt and mountains will be flattened; and all of creation will be on its knees before the Almighty. By Allāh! I am weak in rectifying myself, how then will I be able to rectify others? And if you are truthful in what you say and your state is exactly as you have stated, I will give you the address of a doctor who is an expert at treating those who have broken hearts. He can also cure wounds which are caused by sadness and grief. Listen! That physician is actually Allāh ﷻ. Turn to Him sincerely. Undoubtedly, I cannot have any relationship with you because of these Words of Allāh ﷻ:

وَاَنْذِرْهُمْ يَوْمَ الْاٰزِفَةِ اِذِ الْقُلُوْبُ لَدَى الْحَنَاجِرِ كٰظِمِيْنَ ۬ مَا لِلظّٰلِمِيْنَ مِنْ حَمِيْمٍ وَّلَا
شَفِيْعٍ يُّطَاعُ ۝ يَعْلَمُ خَآئِنَةَ الْاَعْيُنِ وَمَا تُخْفِى الصُّدُوْرُ

And warn them of the day of impending calamity, when hearts will rise up to the throats filled with grief; and the disbelievers will have neither any friend nor any intercessor who will be obeyed. Allāh well knows the covert glance and all what lies hidden in the hearts.

(Sūrah al-Mu'min, 40: 18-19)

Upon reading this, the lady lowered her head and started crying profusely. After composing herself, she looked up and saw that the young man was no longer there. She returned to her home and made it her habit to spend her time in obedience and worship. She would always remain busy in remembrance of Allāh ﷻ. Whenever she would remember the young man she would ask for the letter and place it on her eyes. Once, someone asked her, "What do you get from doing this?" She replied, "What else can I do? Is there any other remedy for me other than this?" She would remain busy in the remembrance of Allāh ﷻ all day long. She would spend her night standing in prayer and spent her whole life in this manner until she left this mortal world.

It has also been reported that the lady contracted a severe illness which resulted in different parts of her body being amputated, otherwise the illness would have spread all over her body. When the physician would amputate a body part, she would experience great pain and would stop him. However, when the young man was mentioned to her, she would feel no pain and the physician was easily able to amputate that body part. Finally, this illness resulted in her death. (Uyūn al-Ḥikāyat, Part 2)

<u>Obscene Lady and Pure Young Man</u>

Ḥaḍrat 'Abdullāh bin Wahab رحمة الله عليه reports from Ḥaḍrat Ibrāhīm رحمة الله عليه:

There was a young man amongst the Banī Isrā'īl who had forsaken the world and would spend all his time in worship, in the remembrance of Allāh ﷻ. Some evil people became jealous and decided that they would find a way to disgrace and shame the young man.

These jealous people spent all their time in trying to think of a way in which they could disgrace and shame the young man. Finally, their evil minds decided that they would bribe and pay a certain woman, who was very beautiful and of loose moral character, to seduce the young man. They approached the woman and said, "If you can seduce the young man, we will make you wealthy because we have faith that you can help us to disgrace and shame him." The lady agreed to this and she went to the young man's place of worship one night. It was a very dark night and it had also started raining. The lady called out to the young man, "O slave of Allāh! Give me shelter." The young man looked down and saw that a young lady was standing at his door asking for permission to enter. The young man thought that allowing a strange woman into his house at this time of the night was very dangerous. He therefore went back inside and started performing prayers. The lady called out again, "O slave of Allāh! It is raining very heavily outside and it is extremely cold. For Allāh's sake! Give me shelter for just one night." The lady kept repeating this until finally, the young man felt sorry for her and allowed her in. He then busied himself in praying his nightly litanies and supplications.

The obscene lady removed her clothing until she was nude. She then came in front of the young man and invited him to engage in sin. The modest young man immediately lowered his gaze and moved away from her. She approached him again and invited him to have relations with her. The young man said, "By Allāh! I will not commit this sin until I test my soul and see that if it commits this sin, is it able to withstand the fire of hell." The young man started walking towards a lamp and placed one of his fingers on the flame until it was burnt. He then carried on with his prayers. The lady approached him again and invited him to sin. He then burnt another of his fingers. In this manner, the lady kept inviting him to sin and he kept burning his fingers. Finally, the young man had burnt all of his fingers but had not looked up at the lady and kept protecting his chastity and honour. When the lady saw that the young man had burnt all of his fingers in order to save himself from this one sin, she let out a loud scream and passed away. (Uyūn al-Ḥikāyat, Part 2)

Read the above incidents again and again and realise how insignificant carnal desires were as far as these people were concerned.

Modesty of Pious Women

Just as modesty is an important quality for men, it is even more important for women. This is why modesty had been emphasised for women many times also. The pious female slaves of Allāh ﷻ have always decorated themselves with this quality. They have left such lasting legacies of their piety that they will be examples for all women until the Day of Judgement.

Modesty Upheld Even During Great Grief

It is reported that a woman named Umme Khallād came with her face covered to the Prophet ﷺ to ask about her son, who had been martyred fighting for Islām. Upon seeing her covered in this manner, one of the companions asked her, 'You have come with your face covered to ask about your son who has been martyred?' She replied, 'My son has passed away and died, my modesty has not died.' (Abū Dāwūd Kitāb al-Jihād, Vol 1. Pg. 336)

The pious slaves of Allāh ﷻ valued modesty more than their lives, as you can see from the above incident. Even though her son had been martyred in battle, Umme Khallād still ensured that she was properly covered and veiled before leaving her home. If we look at our society today, we find that it is completely the opposite. Whether it is a happy occasion or a time of sadness, we see that the principles and orders of Islām are forsaken. Islamic morals and values are completely ignored during happy occasions like weddings and engagements. If someone is experiencing difficulties or a death occurs, mourning and wailing is done in such a manner that modesty and shame are nowhere to be found. Women should use this incident of Ḥaḍrat Umme Khallād as an example of how to retain and display modesty at all times and should resolve to ensure they are covered and veiled always.

Head Covering Ripped

Sayyidunā Alqamah ؓ reports from his mother who narrated that Sayyidah Ḥafṣah bint 'Abd al-Raḥmān ؓ once went to Sayyidah 'Āisha ؓ whilst wearing a thin head covering. Sayyidah 'Āisha ؓ ripped the head covering and gave her a thick head covering to wear. (Mishkāt al-Maṣābīḥ Kitāb al-Libās)

A head covering is a guardian of a woman's dignity and honour. It is the responsibility of women to use the head covering to cover their heads and cover the parts of the body for which the head covering is made. Nowadays, in the name of fashion, head coverings are so thin and transparent that there is no difference whether it is placed on the head or not. Women should ensure that they wear head coverings which properly cover their hair, shoulders and chest areas. We can see how much Sayyidah 'Āisha Ṣiddīqa ﵂ disliked thin head coverings from the above incident.

Veiled Even After Death

When Sayyidah Fāṭimah al-Zahrā ﵂ was close to death, she called Asmā bint al-'Umais ﵂ and said, "I do not like open funeral biers because they do not protect a woman's modesty." Sayyidah Asmā said, "Should I show you the biers I saw in Ethiopia?" After being granted permission, Sayyidah Asmā got some palm tree branches and placed them over the bier, then covered them with a cloth which completely covered the bier and made it impossible to see the body of the deceased. Upon seeing this Sayyidah Fāṭimah ﵂ was extremely pleased and left instructions that she should be taken for burial in this manner. (Asad al-Ghāba, Pg. 524)

This is a supreme example of modesty and veiling of oneself. These ladies had such passion and desire to remain veiled and covered even after they had passed away, whereas the state of the women of this era is not hidden from anyone. Niqāb is worn in order to cover the body and ensure that the gaze of *ghayr maḥram* males does not fall on women; the state nowadays is that fashion has entered into it and such designs are placed on Niqābs that people's attention is attracted towards it, instead of being diverted away from it. Islām ordered women to wear the Niqāb and cover themselves in order to increase their honour and respect and safeguard themselves from wandering eyes. However, the women of today have forsaken this order of Islām thereby making themselves a target for everyone to gaze and stare at (May Allāh protect).

Effect of a Modest Lady's Supplication

A pious person stated:

"I saw an ironmonger taking iron out of the fire with his bare hands. I asked him, 'Why does the fire not burn you?' He replied, 'There was a beautiful woman who lived next door to me who I fell in love with. However, due to her purity and piety, she did not reciprocate my feelings and I was not able to attract her towards me. Then a famine broke out and she came to me looking for some food. I told her what my desire was but she said that she would rather remain hungry than indulge in evil with me. She came to me for five or six days in a row and each time I would offer to give her food in exchange for her fulfilling my desire – but she would return empty-handed rather than give in to my demand.

Finally, after a number of days had passed, out of fear of Allāh ﷻ I gave her some food. She said, 'I will accept this food only if you are giving it to me solely for the sake of Allāh ﷻ. I will remain hungry but will not give in to your demand.' I told her that I was giving it to her solely to seek the pleasure of Allāh ﷻ. She placed the food in front of her and made the following supplication:

اَللّٰهُمَّ اِنْ كَانَ صَادِقًا فَحَرِّمْهُ عَلَى النَّارِ فِي الدُّنْيَا وَالْاٰخِرَةِ وَقَدْ اَجَابَ اللّٰهُ دُعَائَهَا

'O Allāh! If he is truthful then make the fire of this world and the Hereafter forbidden for him.' Her supplication was accepted

And fire does not harm me."

(Nuzhat al-Majālis, Vol. 1, Pg. 103)

The Prophet ﷺ has stated:

مَنْ قَدَرَ عَلٰى اِمْرَاةٍ اَوْ جَارِيَةٍ حَرَامًا فَتَرَكَهَا مَخَافَةً مِّنَ اللّٰهِ اٰمِنَهُ اللّٰهُ مِنَ الْفَزَعِ الْاَكْبَرِ وَحَرَّمَ عَلَيْهِ النَّارَ وَاَدْخَلَهُ الْجَنَّةَ

'A person who has the power and ability to commit a sin with a free woman or slave-girl, but does not out of fear of Allāh ﷻ will be forgiven, he will have the fire of Hell made impermissible on him and he will be entered into Paradise by Allāh ﷻ.

(Nuzhat al-Majālis, Vol. 1, Pg. 103)

Subḥān Allāh! It was the way of the pious and devout ladies that they would be willing to withstand hunger, but would not want to stain their honour and purity. When they protect themselves for the sake of Allāh ﷻ, He raises their status and, through them, forgives and raises the status of others also.

Patch From Pure Clothes

Ḥaḍrat Shaikh 'Abd al-Ḥaqq Muḥaddith al-Dehlwī رحمة الله عليه writes:

'Once, there was a drought. People made lots of supplications but there was no rain. Then Ḥaḍrat Shaikh Nizāmuddīn رحمة الله عليه got a patch from the clothes of his mother and said, 'O Allāh! This is a patch from the clothes of a woman whose clothes have never been seen by a *ghayr maḥram* male. Through the blessings of this patch, grant us rain.' As soon as he completed that sentence, it began to rain.' (Akhbār al-Akhyār, Pg. 40)

Subḥān Allāh! When a patch from the clothes of one who ensures she remains modest and veiled is such that supplicating through it brings about rain, what would the status of the lady who wears such clothes be in the Court of Allāh ﷻ? Many women complain that their supplications are not accepted. They should learn from this incident and realise that if they ensure they are veiled and remain modest, then they will surely see the blessings of that in their lives.

Veiled During Epileptic Fit

Sayyidunā 'Atā bin Rubāḥ رضي الله عنه narrates that Sayyidunā 'Abdullāh bin 'Abbās رضي الله عنهما asked him, 'Should I show you a woman who is a dweller of Paradise?' He replied, 'Please do.' 'Abdullāh bin 'Abbās رضي الله عنهما said, 'That Ethiopian lady standing there.' He then said, 'Once she came to the Prophet ﷺ and said, 'I suffer from epilepsy and during my epileptic fits, some parts of my body sometimes become uncovered. Supplicate to Allāh ﷻ on my behalf.' The Prophet ﷺ said, 'If you display patience, Allāh ﷻ will grant you Paradise as reward for it. And if you want I will supplicate for Allāh ﷻ to grant you cure from your illness.'

The lady said, 'Allāh willing I will be patient, but please supplicate for me that during my epileptic fits, my body does not become uncovered.' The Prophet ﷺ then supplicated for her modesty to be safeguarded during her epileptic fits. (Ṣaḥīḥ al-Bukhārī, Vol. 7, Pg. 166)

Everyone knows that during an epileptic fit, a person does not have control over their body movements, and quite often a person will be rendered unconscious, which can result in parts of the body becoming uncovered. From the above incident, we see the difference between the women of this era and the women of that era. Even during an epileptic fit, women of previous generations would worry about modesty and being covered, whereas women of this generation do not care about modesty and covering up, even whilst they are fully conscious. It is said that the happier the occasion, the more uncovered women become. It is common nowadays during weddings and such, for young ladies and women to dress up and beautify themselves with make-up. They then step outside and display their beauty for all to see. Is this what a modest and honourable woman should do?

A Modest Lady

Ḥaḍrat Abū Hilāl Aswad رحمه الله stated:

"Whilst travelling for pilgrimage, I met a lady who was also going for pilgrimage but she did not have any supplies for her journey. She did not even have any utensil with her for drinking water from. I asked her, "O slave of Allāh! Where are you coming from?" She replied, "Balkh." I asked, "How come you do not have an animal to ride nor any supplies to eat and drink?" She said, "When I left Balkh, I brought ten Dirhams with me. I have spent some of it and have some left." I asked, "What will you do when what you have runs out?" She replied, "I have this extra Jubbah which I will sell." I asked, "What about when that money runs out?" She said, "I will sell my blanket and use that money." I said, "The amount of money that you will get for these things is quite small. What about when the money runs out?" She replied, "Then I will ask my Lord and He will grant me something." I said, "Why do you not ask Him at the outset before selling all your possessions?" She replied, "May Allāh bless you with goodness! I am shy to ask my Merciful Lord for anything whilst I still have extra worldly possessions."

I said to the lady, "O slave of Allāh! Can you take my donkey a little ways away so I can answer the call of nature? I will catch up to you in a few moments." She said, "Okay I will. Leave it here and do not worry." I left the donkey with her and went to answer the call of nature. When I returned, on my donkey was a bag full of delicious foods. I had never seen such food before. In amazement, I looked around but could not see or find the lady anywhere. She had disappeared without a trace in an instant. (Uyūn al-Ḥikāyat, Part 2)

Benefits of Modesty & Chastity

We see a number of benefits of modesty and chastity in this world and the hereafter, which have been mentioned at many places in Aḥādīth.

Modesty Leads to Great Goodness

Sayyidunā ʻImrān bin Ḥuṣayn ﵁ narrates that the Prophet ﷺ said:

اَلْحَيَاءُ لَا يَأْتِي إِلَّا بِخَيْرٍ

Modesty leads to nothing but goodness.

(Ṣaḥīḥ al-Bukhārī, Vol. 8, Pg. 29)

This tells us that a modest person will not be at a loss in this world or the hereafter. He attains success and benefit every step of the way.

In the Shade of the Throne

Sayyidunā Abū Hurairah ﵁ narrates that the Prophet ﷺ said:

سَبْعَةٌ يُظِلُّهُمُ اللهُ فِي ظِلِّهِ يَوْمَ لَا ظِلَّ إِلَّا ظِلُّهُ: اَلْإِمَامُ الْعَادِلُ وَشَابٌّ نَشَأَ فِي عِبَادَةِ رَبِّهِ
وَرَجُلٌ قَلْبُهُ مُعَلَّقٌ فِي الْمَسَاجِدِ وَرَجُلَانِ تَحَابَّا فِي اللهِ اجْتَمَعَا عَلَيْهِ وَتَفَرَّقَا عَلَيْهِ وَرَجُلٌ
طَلَبَتْهُ امْرَأَةٌ ذَاتُ مَنْصِبٍ وَجَمَالٍ فَقَالَ: إِنِّي أَخَافُ اللهَ وَرَجُلٌ تَصَدَّقَ أَخْفَى حَتّٰى لَا تَعْلَمَ
شِمَالُهُ مَا تُنْفِقُ يَمِيْنُهُ وَرَجُلٌ ذَكَرَ اللهَ خَالِيًا فَفَاضَتْ عَيْنَاهُ

There are seven whom Allāh will shade with His Shade on the day when there will be no shade except His: the just ruler; a young man who grows up worshipping his Lord; a man whose heart is attached to the mosque; two men who love one another for the sake of Allāh and meet and part on that basis; a man who is called by a woman of rank and beauty and says 'I fear Allāh'; a man who gives in charity and conceals it to such an extent that his left hand does not know what his right hand gives; and a man who remembers Allāh when he is alone, and his eyes fill up.

(Ṣaḥīḥ al-Bukhārī, Vol. 1, Pg. 33)

The people who will be granted shade includes those who ensure they are modest and remain chaste. Even if a woman of rank and beauty invites them to sin, they control their desires and safeguard themselves from sin. Such a person shall also be granted shade by Allāh ﷻ under the Throne on the Day of Judgement.

Reward for Modesty and Chastity

Modesty and chastity are excellent qualities; in fact, they are a supreme and exalted form of showing obedience to Allāh ﷻ. We also see numerous examples mentioned of the favours which are showered by Allāh ﷻ on a person who has these qualities. Some of them are as follows.

Modesty Rewarded with Power and Authority

After Ḥaḍrat Yusuf ؑ was thrown into the well by his brothers, a passing caravan captured him. They made him a slave and took him to Egypt, where they sold him as a slave. This was a time of great loneliness for Ḥaḍrat Yusuf ؑ as he had no family, friends or acquaintances in Egypt. On the face of it, he appeared to be without a helper or protector. As he got older and became a young man, the wife of the ruler of Egypt, Zuleykhā, invited him to commit sin. Ḥaḍrat Yusuf ؑ sought refuge with Allāh ﷻ and ran out of the room. Zuleykhā falsely accused Ḥaḍrat Yusuf ؑ and had him sent to prison. Sayyidunā Yusuf ؑ put up with the difficulties and troubles of prison life for a number of years. Finally, there came a time when the Mercy of Allāh ﷻ rained down on him and not only was he freed, he was made the treasurer of the land. One who had been a slave a few years earlier, was now the master. Due to his chastity, he received financial rewards in this world and received respect in such a manner that his father and brothers all bowed down before him. In every era and every generation, whoever spends their life in a pure and chaste manner like Sayyidunā Yusuf ؑ, Allāh ﷻ will grant them respect and majesty in this world.

Mouth of the Cave Opened

The story of three men of the Banī Isrā'īl is reported in Ṣaḥīḥ Ḥadīth. Whilst on a journey, it started raining hard and, to escape the rain, they entered into a cave. Due to the rain and storm, a large boulder rolled down and blocked the mouth of the cave. The boulder was so large that the three of them could not move it. There was no other way to escape the cave. The three of them did not know what to do and thought that they would die in this cave. In this stressful, worrying and serious situation, the three of them decided that they would present one of their deeds in the Court of Allāh ﷻ and seek freedom from this difficulty through that deed.

The first man said, "O Allāh! A person did some work for me and left before I was able to pay him. With the money I owed him I bought a goat. Over time, that one goat became a very large herd of goats. After a long time, he came back to be paid for his work. I gave him the whole herd of goats as payment. O Allāh! If this deed of mine is acceptable to You, grant us freedom from this difficulty." The boulder moved a little bit, but not enough for them to be able to get out of the cave.

The second man said, "O Allāh! All through my youth, I was in love with the daughter of my uncle who was very beautiful. I tried many things in order to get close to her but she was very pure and chaste and did not fall for any of my tricks. One time, due to great poverty, she came to me to ask for a loan. I promised to give her money on the condition that she would fulfil my desire. She was desperate and agreed to my condition. When I approached her to have relations, she said, "Fear Allāh ﷻ and do not break this seal." Her words struck me like lightning and fear of Allāh ﷻ overcame me. I gave her the money and did not have any relations with her. O Allāh! If this deed of mine is acceptable in Your Court, grant us freedom from this difficulty." The boulder moved a little bit more, but not enough for them to be able to get out of the cave.

The third man said, "I served my mother and father dutifully. I would present milk to my mother and then go to sleep. One day, when I came with the milk my mother had fallen asleep. I did not think it appropriate to wake her and stood there with the milk in my hand until she woke up on her own. I stood there all night until it was morning. O Allāh! Accept this deed of mine and grant us freedom from this difficulty." The boulder moved completely away from the mouth of the cave and the three of them were able to escape. (Ṣaḥīḥ al-Bukhārī, Vol. 3, Pg. 91)

In this incident, the deed of the second person was regarding purity and chastity. That deed of his was accepted by Allāh ﷻ and the blessings of it granted them freedom from their difficulty.

Principles and Rules of Modesty

Allāh ﷻ has declared a husband and wife to be the clothing of each other and has stated in the Qur'ān:

$$هُنَّ لِبَاسٌ لَكُمْ وَأَنْتُمْ لِبَاسٌ لَهُنَّ$$

They are coverings for you and you are coverings for them;
(Sūrah al-Baqarah, 2: 187)

Islām desires that all the beauty, splendour and elegance of a woman is only shared with her husband. It does not want any other male to see the beauty which is reserved for her husband. The adornment and decoration of a woman should be done only for her husband. A wife has been made a source of comfort for a husband. Allāh ﷻ states:

$$وَمِنْ اٰيٰتِهٖٓ اَنْ خَلَقَ لَكُمْ مِّنْ اَنْفُسِكُمْ اَزْوَاجًا لِّتَسْكُنُوْٓا اِلَيْهَا وَجَعَلَ بَيْنَكُمْ مَّوَدَّةً وَّرَحْمَةً$$

And among His signs is that He created spouses for you from yourselves for you to gain rest from them, and kept love and mercy between yourselves;
(Sūrah al-Rūm, 30: 21)

If you look at it, a woman beautifies and adorns herself in order to focus her husband's attention towards her. Islām is the only religion which also puts restrictions on natural instincts and has emphasised that the attraction between a man and a woman, and the natural instinct to be with one another, should only be done in a lawful manner. The beauty and elegance of a woman has been restricted by Allāh ﷻ Who has stated that it is only for the husband, so that all his attention is focused on her and she is safeguarded from the desires and eyes of other males.

There are two stages of the Islamic ruling for covering oneself. The first is the ruling for inside the home and the orders for this have been mentioned in Sūrah al-Nūr; this is for *Satr*. The second is the ruling for outside the home and the orders for this have been mentioned in Sūrah al-Aḥzāb; and this is the ruling for *Ḥijāb*.

Difference Between Satr and Ḥijāb

In terms of covering oneself, many people do not differentiate between *satr* and *ḥijāb*, whereas the Islamic rules are different for each of them. *Satr* is that part of the body which must always be covered in front of other people. It is only permissible for a husband and wife to view each other's *satr*. The *satr* for a man is from the navel to the knees and for a woman it is the whole body except for the hands, feet and face. Under normal circumstances, a woman is not allowed to show any of her *satr* to any man except for her husband.

Ḥijāb is the covering which must be worn if a woman has to leave the home for any reason. At such a time, a woman must cover herself in the manner which Islām has stated when going in front of *ghayr maḥram* males. The order for *ḥijāb* has been mentioned in Sūrah al-Aḥzāb. What it states is that when a woman leaves the home she should wear a *Jilbāb* (*Abāya*), or a large covering so that her whole body is covered and that her face should be covered with a *Niqāb* so that only the eyes are visible. Therefore, *ḥijāb* means that other than the eyes, the whole body shall be covered.

Order for Covering Oneself

It is important to understand the orders that Islām has given for covering oneself. Let us look at them in detail:

1) **Seek permission when entering someone's home**

Allāh states:

يَٰٓأَيُّهَا ٱلَّذِينَ ءَامَنُوا لَا تَدْخُلُوا بُيُوتًا غَيْرَ بُيُوتِكُمْ حَتَّىٰ تَسْتَأْنِسُوا وَتُسَلِّمُوا

عَلَىٰٓ أَهْلِهَا ۚ ذَٰلِكُمْ خَيْرٌ لَّكُمْ لَعَلَّكُمْ تَذَكَّرُونَ ﴿٢٧﴾ فَإِن لَّمْ تَجِدُوا فِيهَآ أَحَدًا

فَلَا تَدْخُلُوهَا حَتَّىٰ يُؤْذَنَ لَكُمْ ۖ وَإِن قِيلَ لَكُمُ ٱرْجِعُوا

فَٱرْجِعُوا هُوَ أَزْكَىٰ لَكُمْ ۚ وَٱللَّهُ بِمَا تَعْمَلُونَ عَلِيمٌ ﴿٢٨﴾

O People who believe! Do not enter the houses except your own until you obtain permission and have conveyed peace upon its inhabitants; this is better for you, in order that you may ponder. And if you do not

find anyone in them, even then do not enter without the permission of their owners; and if it is said to you, "Go away" then go away – this is much purer for you; and Allāh knows your deeds.
(Sūrah al-Nūr, 24: 27-28)

Ṣadr al-Afāḍil, Ḥaḍrat 'Allāma Na'īmuddīn Murādabādī رحمۃ اللہ علیہ writes:

'This verse proves that it is not allowed to enter another person's home without permission. Another method of obtaining permission to enter is to say 'Subḥān Allāh, Alḥamdulillāh, Allāhu Akbar' or to cough etc., which would indicate to the home owners that someone wishes to enter. Or a person could say, "May I have permission to enter?" The home of another means a house in which a person lives, regardless of whether they own that house or not. If you see the person whose house you are going to before reaching the house, you should greet him first and then ask for permission to go to his house. If he is inside his house, he should be greeted and permission should be sought to enter at the same time, by saying 'Assalāmu 'Alaikum, may I enter?' It is stated in a Ḥadīth to greet before talking. It has also been stated to seek permission and then greet.'
(Madārik, Kashāf, Aḥmadī)

Rule: If, by standing directly in front of the door, there is a danger of seeing inside the house, then one should stand slightly to the left or right when greeting and seeking permission.

Rule: It is stated in Ḥadīth that even if one's mother is in the home, permission should be sought before entering. (Muwaṭṭa Imām Mālik)

We also realise from the verse that to knock very hard or to shout loudly to seek permission, especially at the homes of scholars and the pious, is disliked and against proper etiquettes. (Khazāin al-'Irfān)

It is also stated in the Qur'ān:

يٰٓاَيُّهَا الَّذِيْنَ اٰمَنُوْا لِيَسْتَاْذِنْكُمُ الَّذِيْنَ مَلَكَتْ اَيْمَانُكُمْ وَالَّذِيْنَ لَمْ يَبْلُغُوا الْحُلُمَ
مِنْكُمْ ثَلٰثَ مَرّٰتٍ مِنْ قَبْلِ صَلٰوةِ الْفَجْرِ وَحِيْنَ تَضَعُوْنَ ثِيَابَكُمْ مِّنَ الظَّهِيْرَةِ
وَمِنْ بَعْدِ صَلٰوةِ الْعِشَآءِ

O People who believe! The slaves you possess and those among you who have not attained adulthood, must seek your permission on three occasions; before the dawn prayer, and when you remove your garments in the afternoon, and after the night prayer;

(Sūrah al-Nūr, 24: 58)

This means that on occasions when a husband and wife would normally be alone, slaves or children should not enter their rooms without permission.

- It was the habit of the Prophet ﷺ that when he would go to someone's house, he ﷺ would not stand directly in front of the door. Because in those days there was no covering on the front door. He ﷺ would stand to the right or left of the door and then seek permission to enter. (Sunan Abū Dāwūd)

Scholars have stated that it is also necessary for blind people to seek permission to enter so that there is no risk of them overhearing the conversation of the people in the home.

- Permission should be asked a maximum of three times; this was the habit of the Prophet ﷺ and this is the limit he stipulated. If no reply is received after the third time, a person should return home. (Ṣaḥīḥ al-Bukhārī, Ṣaḥīḥ al-Muslim)

- A person came to the home of the Prophet ﷺ and stood directly in front of the door when asking for permission to enter. The Prophet ﷺ said, "What is this you are doing? The reason for asking for permission to enter is so that your gaze does not fall on anything inside the home." (Sunan Abū Dāwūd)

- Ḥaḍrat Thaubān ؓ narrates that the Prophet ﷺ said, "When your gaze has entered (the home), what is the need to seek permission to enter the home yourself?" (Sunan Abū Dāwūd)

- A person came to the home of the Prophet ﷺ and said, "Can I come in?" The Prophet ﷺ said to his slave, "This person does not know the manner of seeking permission to enter. Go and inform him that the manner of seeking permission is to say 'Assalāmu Alaikum, may I enter?'" (Sunan Abū Dāwūd)

- Ḥaḍrat Kaldah bin Ḥanbal went to the Prophet ﷺ on a particular matter and sat down without any greeting. The Prophet ﷺ said, "Go back outside, say 'Assalāmu Alaikum' and then enter." (Sunan Abū Dāwūd)

- Ḥaḍrat Jābir bin 'Abdullāh ؓ states: "I went to the home of the Prophet ﷺ and knocked on the door. The Prophet ﷺ asked, "Who is it?" I replied, "It is me." The Prophet ﷺ disapprovingly said, "It is me, it is me?" (Meaning that he ﷺ disliked the response).

  The response of the Prophet ﷺ showed that he disapproved of the response and is an indication that upon being asked, the person seeking permission should state their name so that the homeowner is aware of who is seeking permission to enter. The homeowner can then decide if permission should be given or not.

Seek Permission When Entering Your Own Home

- A person asked the Prophet ﷺ, "Do I need to ask for permission when I go to visit my mother?" The Prophet ﷺ replied, "Yes." He said, "She has no one other than me to serve her. Do I need to seek permission each time I go to serve her?" The Prophet ﷺ said, "Would you like it if you saw your mother naked?" (Ibn Jarīr)

- Ḥaḍrat 'Abdullāh ibn Mas'ūd ؓ stated, "Seek permission even when visiting your mothers and sisters." His wife, Ḥaḍrat Zainab, reports that when he would come home he would speak in such a manner that his arrival would be known. (Tafsīr Ibn Kathīr)

2) Keep the Gaze Lowered

Allāh ﷻ has stated:

قُلْ لِّلْمُؤْمِنِيْنَ يَغُضُّوْا مِنْ اَبْصَارِهِمْ وَيَحْفَظُوْا فُرُوْجَهُمْ ؕ

Command the Muslim men to keep their gaze low and to protect their private organs; that is much purer for them;

(Sūrah al-Nūr, 24: 58)

In the following verse, Allāh ﷻ states:

وَقُلْ لِّلْمُؤْمِنٰتِ يَغْضُضْنَ مِنْ اَبْصَارِهِنَّ وَيَحْفَظْنَ فُرُوْجَهُنَّ وَلَا يُبْدِيْنَ زِيْنَتَهُنَّ اِلَّا مَا ظَهَرَ
مِنْهَا وَلْيَضْرِبْنَ بِخُمُرِهِنَّ عَلٰى جُيُوْبِهِنَّ ۖ وَلَا يُبْدِيْنَ زِيْنَتَهُنَّ اِلَّا لِبُعُوْلَتِهِنَّ اَوْ اٰبَآئِهِنَّ اَوْ
اٰبَآءِ بُعُوْلَتِهِنَّ اَوْ اَبْنَآئِهِنَّ اَوْ اَبْنَآءِ بُعُوْلَتِهِنَّ اَوْ اِخْوَانِهِنَّ اَوْ بَنِيْٓ اِخْوَانِهِنَّ اَوْ بَنِيْٓ اَخَوٰتِهِنَّ اَوْ
نِسَآئِهِنَّ اَوْ مَا مَلَكَتْ اَيْمَانُهُنَّ اَوِ التّٰبِعِيْنَ غَيْرِ اُولِي الْاِرْبَةِ مِنَ الرِّجَالِ اَوِ الطِّفْلِ الَّذِيْنَ
لَمْ يَظْهَرُوْا عَلٰى عَوْرٰتِ النِّسَآءِ ۖ وَلَا يَضْرِبْنَ بِاَرْجُلِهِنَّ لِيُعْلَمَ مَا يُخْفِيْنَ مِنْ زِيْنَتِهِنَّ ؕ
وَتُوْبُوْٓا اِلَى اللّٰهِ جَمِيْعًا اَيُّهَ الْمُؤْمِنُوْنَ لَعَلَّكُمْ تُفْلِحُوْنَ

And command the Muslim women to keep their gaze low and to protect their chastity, and not to reveal their adornment except what is apparent, and to keep the cover wrapped over their bosoms; and not to reveal their adornment except to their own husbands or fathers or husbands' fathers, or their sons or their husbands' sons, or their brothers or their brothers' sons or sisters' sons, or women of their religion, or the bondwomen they possess, or male servants provided they do not have manliness, or such children who do not know of women's nakedness, and not to stamp their feet on the ground in order that their hidden adornment be known; and O Muslims, all of you turn in repentance together towards Allāh, in the hope of attaining success.

(Sūrah al-Nūr, 24: 31)

The order to keep the gaze lowered is also for outside the home so that the gaze does not fall on *ghayr maḥram* members of the opposite sex; the same rule and order is also for inside the home. Even inside the home, related women (*maḥram*) should not be stared at unduly. Without a doubt, there is a sacred relationship between men and women who are related. However, due to the fact that they are different genders, there is a natural attraction between the sexes and careless glances can lead to strife and tribulation. The reality is that these evil glances are the first step to indecency. This is why, in these verses, safeguarding the eyes has been mentioned with such importance alongside protecting one's private organs and chastity.

It is reported that a when a blind Companion, Ḥaḍrat 'Abdullāh bin Umme Maktūm ؓ came to the home of the Prophet ﷺ, he ﷺ asked Ḥaḍrat 'Āisha Ṣiddīqa ؓ and Ḥaḍrat Umme Salamah ؓ to cover themselves. They said, "But he is blind." The Prophet ﷺ said, "But you are not blind." (Jāmi' al-Tirmidhī, Vol. 4, Pg. 399)

Our society and culture has reached such a state nowadays that we have given full permission to our daughters to attend various educational institutions, offices and gatherings and mix freely with *ghayr maḥram* males. Some parents say that we trust our daughter. Did the Prophet ﷺ not trust Sayyidah 'Āisha Ṣiddīqa ؓ *(M'ādhAllāh)*, whose purity was testified to by Allāh ﷻ in Sūrah al-Nūr? It is through these glances that shaiṭān enters the body through the eyes and places himself (and his evil temptations) into the heart. Then both parties start to talk and things progress from there. Safeguarding the gaze does not merely mean that men and women should not look at each other's faces. Rather, it also means that they should not look at each other's bodies nor should any indecent pictures or movies be looked at. Guidance on this is provided in the following Aḥādīth:

➤ The Prophet ﷺ said, "O 'Alī! Do not follow the first glance with another. You will be forgiven for the first (which falls accidently), but not for the second." (Jāmi' al-Tirmidhī, Vol. 4, Pg. 398)

➤ Sayyidunā Jarīr bin 'Abdullāh ؓ reports that he asked the Prophet ﷺ, "What should I do if my gaze suddenly falls on someone?" He replied, "Immediately turn away your gaze or look down." (Ṣaḥīḥ al-Muslim, Vol. 3, Pg. 1699)

➤ If the gaze of a person falls on the beauty of a woman and he moves his gaze away, Allāh ﷻ increases the pleasure and enjoyment he experiences in his worship. (Musnad Aḥmad)

➤ Allāh ﷻ has stated, "The sight is one of the poisonous arrows of the devil. Whoever safeguards it out of fear of Me, I will grant him such sweetness of faith that he will taste it in his heart." (Mu'jam al-Kabīr lil-Ṭabarānī, Vol. 2, Pg. 173)

Strict Orders Not To Gaze at the Private Parts of Others

➤ A man should not look at the private parts of another man and a woman should not look at the private parts of another woman. (Ṣaḥīḥ al-Muslim, Vol. 1, Pg. 266)

➤ Ḥaḍrat Sayyidunā 'Alī ⬥ narrates that the Prophet ﷺ said to him, "Do not look at the groin area of any living or deceased person." (Sunan Abū Dāwūd, Vol. 3, Pg. 196)

3) Safeguard the Private Parts

In verses 30 and 31 of Sūrah al-Nūr, which have been previously mentioned, both men and women are instructed to safeguard their private parts. Safeguarding the private parts means two things. The first is that they should safeguard themselves from indecency, fornication, adultery and protect their chastity and honour. The second is that they should not expose their private parts in front of anyone else. Further explanation of this is found in the following Aḥādīth:

➤ The Prophet ﷺ said, "Keep your private parts safeguarded from everyone except for your wife and slave-girl." A person asked, "What about when we are alone?" The Prophet ﷺ replied. "Allāh ﷻ is more deserving of your modesty." (Jāmi' al-Tirmidhī, Vol. 5, Pg. 110)

➤ Sayyidah 'Āisha Ṣiddīqa ⬥ reports that her sister Ḥaḍrat Asmā came to the Prophet ﷺ while wearing thin clothing. The Prophet ﷺ turned away and said, "O Asmā! When a woman reaches puberty, it is not permissible that, except for her hands and face, any part of her body be seen." (Abū Dāwūd, Vol. 4, Pg. 62)

➤ The Prophet ﷺ said, "Allāh's curse is on those women, who despite being clothed, are naked." In explaining this Ḥadīth, Sayyidunā 'Umar al-Fārūq ⬥ stated, "Do not clothe your women in such clothing that the shape of their body can be seen."

> Ḥaḍrat Ḥafṣa bint 'Abd al-Raḥmān 🕮 came to Sayyidah 'Āisha Ṣiddīqa 🕮 while wearing a thin head-covering. Sayyidah 'Āisha ripped it and covered her head in a thicker one. (Muwaṭṭa Imām Mālik, Vol. 2, Pg. 84)

4) Cover the Chest

In the verse of Sūrah al-Nūr mentioned previously, women have been ordered – 'to keep the cover wrapped over their bosoms;' In other words, a veil or some form of clothing should be used to cover the chest area.

Sayyidah 'Āisha Ṣiddīqa 🕮 stated, "After Sūrah al-Nūr was revealed, when the people returned home after hearing it from the Prophet 🕮, they recited the verses to their wives, daughters and sisters. When the women heard these verses, they immediately took additional clothing and covered their heads and chests. The next morning, all the women who came to the Mosque for prayers, had head coverings on which also covered the chest." (Tafsīr Ibn Abī Ḥātim, Vol. 8, Pg. 2575)

5) Women Should Keep Beauty and Adornments Hidden

One of the other orders given to women in the verse of Sūrah al-Nūr mentioned previously is 'not to reveal their adornment except what is apparent.'

In other words, women should not allow their beauty and adornments to be displayed in front of ghayr maḥram males. Except for the adornments which are apparent or which become displayed by themselves. Adornments means the parts of the body which attract men, or where jewellery or other attractive items are worn. The verse further clarifies that women are allowed to display their beauty and adornments in front of those specific people with whom there is no danger of tribulations.

We learn from this verse that other than the husband, a woman is allowed to display her beauty and adornments in front of those people with whom marriage is impermissible. The wisdom of this permission is so that there is no difficulty or inconvenience in working and moving around the home. This verse does not mention a maternal uncle (Māmū) or paternal uncle (*Chācha*); however, they are both mentioned as *maḥram* in verse 23 of Sūrah al-Nisā'. In the same manner, paternal grandfathers, maternal grandfathers, grandchildren and foster brothers are included amongst those who are *maḥram*.

Covering Oneself in Front of a Brother in Law

An important point worth noting is that in the verse mentioned previously, the list of permissible males includes the husband's father and husband's son, but does not include the husband's brother. When this verse was revealed, the Prophet ﷺ was asked if veiling should be done in front of a brother-in-law also. He replied, "Yes! The brother-in-law is death." (Ṣaḥīḥ al-Bukhārī, Vol. 7, Pg. 37)

The wisdom in being ordered to cover oneself is to reduce the possibility of adultery or fornication. In this regard, the most danger to a woman is from those men who are present in the home, or who come and go from the home easily. That is why the Prophet ﷺ said that the younger or older brother of a husband is like death for a wife.

Women Should Cover Themselves From Other Women

This verse also states that women can be uncovered in front of other pious and obedient Muslim women. However, it does not state that they can be uncovered in front of all women. Muslim women should be covered in front of non-Muslim and unfamiliar women because their morals, habits, speech, manners and fashion sense may have an adverse effect on them.

6) **Mixed Gatherings Forbidden**

In the previously mentioned verse, by being forbidden to display adornments in front of unrelated males, Allāh ﷻ has made it forbidden to participate in mixed gatherings with *ghayr maḥram* males. The Prophet ﷺ has stated, "The person who believes in Allāh and the final day should not be alone with a woman without a guardian present because in that situation, the third with them is the devil." (Musnad Imām Aḥmad, Vol. 33, Pg. 19)

The Prophet ﷺ expressed extreme dislike that a man should touch or shake hands with a *ghayr maḥram* female. It is stated in one Ḥadīth, "It is better for an iron rod to be driven into the head of a man, than for him to touch a woman who is not permissible for him."

It is reported in Sunan Nasā'ī and Sunan Ibn Mājah that when the Prophet ﷺ would accept an oath of allegiance (*Bay'at*) from women, he ﷺ would not shake hands with them, he ﷺ would only ask them to say it verbally.

The most obvious display of the forbiddance of mixed gatherings, which Islām has ordered, is at the time of a marriage ceremony. A marriage (*Nikāḥ*) is such a strong agreement between a man and a woman, that it is for life. However, even during the execution of this agreement, one of the signatories of this agreement, namely the woman, is not allowed to be present in front of *ghayr maḥram* males. The permission of the woman is given to the person performing the marriage ceremony by a guardian and two witnesses.

7) Women Should Keep All Jewellery Hidden

The verse of Sūrah al-Nūr also tells women, '***not to stamp their feet on the ground in order that their hidden adornment be known***.'

The Prophet ﷺ did not limit jewellery and adornments to those things which are shiny and expensive, rather he forbade all things which could stir the emotions or attract the attention of men. The following have been mentioned in this regard:

- The appropriate perfume (*'Iṭr*) for men is that which is strong in smell and light in colour, and the appropriate perfume for women is that which is strong in colour and light in smell. (Abū Dāwūd, Vol. 4, Pg. 48)
- A woman who puts on perfume and then walks amongst (unfamiliar) people is an immoral type of woman. (Jāmi' al-Tirmidhī, Vol. 5, Pg. 106)

- If a woman puts on perfume and passes by people so that they can smell her fragrance, she is a 'such and such.' (He used very strong and disparaging words). (Abū Dāwūd, Vol. 4, Pg. 79)

- A woman left the Mosque and was heading home when she passed by Ḥaḍrat Abū Hurairah ؓ, who noticed that she had perfume on. He stopped her and asked, "O slave of Allāh! Are you coming from the Mosque?" She replied that she was. He said, "I have heard my beloved Abū al-Qāsim ﷺ say that the prayer of the woman who comes to the mosque with perfume on will not be accepted until she returns home and has a bath as one has when they are impure." (Abū Dāwūd, Vol. 4, Pg. 79)

- If the Imām forgets something in Ṣalāh, men are ordered to say Subḥān Allāh to make him aware of his mistake. However, women have been told to tap one hand on the back of the other in order to let the Imām know of his mistake. (Ṣaḥīḥ al-Bukhārī, Vol. 1, Pg. 137)

Order of Ḥijāb

The order to cover oneself outside the home has been given in Sūrah al-Aḥzāb. In those orders, the wives of the Prophet ﷺ are being addressed, however the ruling applies to all believing women. The Qur'ān adopted this manner because for men, the Prophet ﷺ is the best example in all matters. However, because of their female gender, the best examples for women are the blessed wives of the Prophet ﷺ. Even though the blessed wives are being addressed directly in those verses, through them the order is being given to all Muslim women.

1) Avoid Talking in a Soft Tone

Allāh ﷻ states in Sūrah al-Aḥzāb:

يٰنِسَآءَ النَّبِيِّ لَسْتُنَّ كَاَحَدٍ مِّنَ النِّسَآءِ اِنِ اتَّقَيْتُنَّ فَلَا تَخْضَعْنَ بِالْقَوْلِ فَيَطْمَعَ الَّذِيْ فِيْ
قَلْبِهٖ مَرَضٌ وَّقُلْنَ قَوْلًا مَّعْرُوْفًا

O the wives of the Prophet! You are not like other women – if you really fear Allāh, do not speak softly lest the one in whose heart is a disease have any inclination, and speak fairly.

(Sūrah al-Aḥzāb, 33: 32)

In other words, if a woman needs to speak to a *ghayr maḥram* male for any reason, she should do so in a straightforward manner and dry tone. There should be no sweetness or attraction in her voice so that the listener is not under any false impressions.

2) Do Not Leave the Home Unnecessarily

It is also stated in Sūrah al-Aḥzāb:

وَقَرْنَ فِي بُيُوتِكُنَّ وَلَا تَبَرَّجْنَ تَبَرُّجَ الْجَاهِلِيَّةِ الْأُولَى

And remain in your houses and do not unveil yourselves like the unveiling prevalent in the times of ignorance.

(Sūrah al-Aḥzāb, 33: 33)

From this verse we learn that it is preferred for a woman to spend her time peacefully and respectfully in her home. In reality, Islām has placed the responsibility for carrying out all the matters outside the home on men. Women have been given responsibility for all affairs inside the home. The differences in responsibilities given to men and women are based on their nature and abilities. This determination has been made by the Lord of the worlds Himself ﷻ, whose wisdom and knowledge cannot be doubted by anyone. He is the Knower of all hidden things and nothing is hidden from His divine vision.

It is correct that there are women who, based on their nature and intelligence, are the equal of or better than some men. There are also some men who, based on their character and nature, are like women. However, it must always be remembered that laws and rules are made for the majority. Allāh ﷻ is the Lord and Creator of all and knows the strengths and weaknesses of everyone. Therefore, the right to make this decision also rests with Him alone. Our duty is to accept His decision and to remain obedient to Him ﷻ.

Islām has freed women from outside responsibilities and has made them responsible for matters inside the home. Let us look at the following Aḥādīth in this regard:

- Verily a woman deserves to be hidden. When she leaves the home the devil stares at her; she is closest to the Mercy of her Lord when she is in an interior part of her home. (Jāmi' al-Tirmidhī, Vol. 2, Pg. 467)
- A woman is the guardian of her husband's home and is responsible for her children. (Jāmi' al-Tirmidhī, Vol. 3, Pg. 260)
- Everyone is aware of the importance and excellence of Jumu'ah and congregational prayers. However, the Prophet ﷺ exempted women from Jumu'ah prayers. He ﷺ has stated, "Performing the Jumu'ah prayer with congregation is obligatory on every Muslim, but four are exempted – slaves, women, children and the sick." (Abū Dāwūd, Vol. 1, Pg. 280)
- Ḥaḍrat Anas رضي الله عنه narrates that some women asked the Prophet ﷺ, "The men are taking all the rewards and merits. They go for Jihād and many other things in the Way of Allāh. What deed can we do whereby we can attain the same rewards?" The Prophet ﷺ replied, "Whichever one of you who remains at home (so you can guard over your husband's possessions, children and honour) will receive the same reward as one who goes out to fight in the way of Allāh." (Ṣaḥīḥ al-Bukhārī)

Can a Woman Leave the Home At All?

Even though a woman's responsibilities are inside the home, it is not completely forbidden for her to leave her house. She is allowed to leave the home for any urgent need or requirement. The Prophet ﷺ said, "Allāh has granted you permission to leave your homes to tend to your needs." (Ṣaḥīḥ al-Bukhārī)

However, they have been ordered to '***not unveil yourselves like the unveiling prevalent in the times of ignorance***.' The word used in this verse is 'تَبَرُّج', which means to 'be prominent', 'noticeable' and 'obvious' etc. For a woman, 'تَبَرُّج' means to display her beauty openly, display her clothing and jewellery openly and to walk and talk in such a manner that she is noticed by others. This means that when a woman steps outside, she should not make herself obvious to people. Rather, she should cover herself well and avoid the gaze of others.

3) Men Should Talk From Behind a Veil

Allāh ﷻ states:

وَاِذَا سَاَلْتُمُوْهُنَّ مَتَاعًا فَسْـَٔلُوْهُنَّ مِنْ وَّرَآءِ حِجَابٍ ذٰلِكُمْ اَطْهَرُ لِقُلُوْبِكُمْ وَ قُلُوْبِهِنَّ

And when you ask the wives of the Prophet for anything to use, ask for it from behind a curtain; this is purer for your hearts and for their hearts;

(Sūrah al-Aḥzāb, 33: 53)

It is not permissible for a male to speak to a *ghayr maḥram* female without a valid reason. However, even if there is a need to speak to her, there is no permission to speak with her face to face. This order was given in relation to the blessed wives of the Prophet ﷺ, with whom Muslims have a sacred and blessed relationship as they do with their real mothers. How then would it be permissible to have face to face conversations or idle chats with normal Muslim women who are not related?

4) Veiling the Face

Allāh ﷻ has stated:

يٰۤاَيُّهَا النَّبِيُّ قُلْ لِّاَزْوَاجِكَ وَبَنٰتِكَ وَنِسَآءِ الْمُؤْمِنِيْنَ يُدْنِيْنَ عَلَيْهِنَّ مِنْ جَلَابِيْبِهِنَّ ؕ
ذٰلِكَ اَدْنٰۤى اَنْ يُّعْرَفْنَ فَلَا يُؤْذَيْنَ

O Prophet! Command your wives and your daughters and the women of the Muslims to cover their faces with a part of their cloaks; this is closer to their being recognised and not being harassed;

(Sūrah al-Aḥzāb, 33: 59)

In this verse, the word 'جَلَابِيْب' is used and is the plural of '*Jilbāb.*' *Jilbāb* is a large cloth which covers the whole body. What this means is that the body should be completely covered and a part of the cloth should be used to cover the head and face. This is to ensure that along with the body, the beauty of the face is also covered, however, the eyes can remain visible.

From the following Aḥādīth, we can see the extent to which this order was acted upon during the time of the Prophet ﷺ.

- In relation to the incident of Ifak (when 'Abdullāh bin Ubai slandered Sayyidah 'Āisha Ṣiddīqa رضي الله عنها), she states, "When I came back from answering the call of nature, I saw that the caravan and whole group had left. I sat down and was so tired that I fell asleep. In the morning, Ḥaḍrat Ṣafwān bin Mu'ṭal passed by and saw someone laying on the ground from a distance. He approached and, upon seeing me, he recognised me for he had seen me before the order for covering the face was revealed. When he said, 'إِنَّا لِلَّهِ وَإِنَّا إِلَيْهِ رَاجِعُونَ', I woke up and I quickly covered my face with my cloth." The words of the Ḥadīth which indicate she covered her face are 'فَخَمَّرْتُ وَجْهِي بِجِلْبَابِي'. (Ṣaḥīḥ al-Bukhārī, Vol. 5, Pg. 116)

- As has been mentioned earlier, a woman named Umme Khallād came with her face covered to the Prophet ﷺ to ask about her son, who had been martyred fighting for Islām. Upon seeing her covered in this manner, one of the companions asked her, 'You have come with your face covered to ask about your son who has been martyred?' She replied, 'My son has passed away and died, my modesty has not died.' The Prophet ﷺ then consoled her and said, "You son will receive the reward of two martyrs." She asked why that was the case. The Prophet ﷺ said, "That is because he has been killed by the people of the Book." (Abū Dāwūd, Vol. 3, Pg. 5)

- In relation to the journey to perform the farewell pilgrimage, Sayyidah 'Āisha Ṣiddīqa رضي الله عنها reports, "Groups of people would pass by us and we were with the Prophet ﷺ in a state of *Iḥrām*. When the group would get close to us, we would take a large cloth and place it in front of our faces and after they had passed, we would remove the cloth." (Abū Dāwūd, Vol. 2, Pg. 167)

- Sayyidunā 'Abdullāh bin 'Abbās رضي الله عنهما narrates that on the journey back from the farewell pilgrimage, the cousin of the Prophet ﷺ, Ḥaḍrat Faḍl bin 'Abbās (who was still a youngster at this time), was riding with him on his camel. During the journey, when some women passed by, Faḍl bin 'Abbās started looking at them. The Prophet ﷺ placed his hand on the face of Faḍl bin 'Abbās and moved it away. (Abū Dāwūd, Vol. 2, Pg. 161)

Restrictions on Looking

There is no doubt that the life of a person is closely connected with vision and sight. Education, business, friendship, enmity, marriage and all interactions require sight and vision. This sight plays an important role when making any decision. A person cannot protect himself from the effects of what is seen by his eyes and heard by his ears. Seeing a beautiful garden or water bubbling from a spring or any other natural beauty fills the heart with pleasure and delight. Seeing an offensive or abominable sight fills one with unhappiness and sadness. How then is it possible for a person to see a beautiful young female and not be excited in his heart? This is why Islām has also restrained and controlled the eyes and Muslim men and women have been ordered to keep their gaze lowered. Along with this, every action of a woman has been restricted which would invite men to look at them.

Sayyidunā 'Abdullāh bin Mas'ūd ﷺ narrates that the Prophet ﷺ said that Allāh ﷻ stated:

إِنَّ النَّظْرَةَ سَهْمٌ مِنْ سِهَامِ إِبْلِيسَ مَسْمُومٌ مَنْ تَرَكَهَا مَخَافَتِي أَبْدَلْتُهُ إِيمَانًا يَجِدُ حَلَاوَتَهُ فِي قَلْبِهِ

Verily looking at one who is *ghayr maḥram* is one of the poisonous arrows of the devil. Whoever safeguards it out of fear of Me, I will grant him such sweetness of faith that he will taste it in his heart.

(Al-Mu'jam al-Kabīr lil-Ṭabarānī, Vol. 10, Pg. 173)

Just as there is restriction on males looking at females, there is a similar restriction on females looking at males.

Speaking With *Ghayr Mahram* People

Even though it is not explicitly forbidden for *ghayr maḥram* men and women to speak with one another, idle chatting, laughing and joking (with each other) have been strictly prohibited. If it is necessary to speak to them, care should be taken to ensure that the manner of speech is not attractive or appealing. The conversation should take place from behind a curtain and should only take place if it is extremely necessary. Along with this, it is necessary to remember that the conversation should not be in private, because when a man and woman are alone, the third with them is the devil who places temptations in their hearts.

Forbidden to Touch *Ghayr Maḥram* People

Any form of touching a *ghayr maḥram* person, even if it is only for a moment, has been declared unlawful and impermissible. Touching a *ghayr maḥram* person is a grave sin in the eyes of Islām.

Sayyidunā Abū Hurairah ؓ and Sayyidunā 'Abdullāh ibn 'Abbās ؓ narrate that the Prophet ﷺ said:

مَنْ صَافَحَ امْرَاَةً حَرَامًا جَاءَ يَوْمَ الْقِيَامَةِ مَغْلُولَةً يَدَاهُ اِلٰى عُنُقِهٖ ثُمَّ يُؤْمَرُ بِهٖ اِلَى النَّارِ

Whoever shakes hands with a *ghayr maḥram* woman will be brought on the Day of Judgement in such a manner that both his arms will be wrapped around his neck and the order will be given to throw him into the fire.

(Musnad al-Ḥārith, Pg. 309)

Mixed Gatherings

Islām has also placed restrictions on mixed gatherings of men and women because indecency generally starts from gatherings like these. In the same way, free mixing of boys and girls [who have reached puberty] in schools and colleges, as well as men and women mixing freely in offices have also been restricted by Islām.

These restrictions have also been placed due to the fact that men and women mixing freely will almost always give rise to temptations, tribulations and an increase in shamelessness and immodesty.

A Man and Woman Meeting in Private

If a man and woman who are not related meet in private, it is possible that they give in to the whispers of the devil, even if they are pure and chaste. Their firm and pure intentions may waver and be ruined. They could become trapped in the evil plans of the devil and become embroiled in impermissible acts. This is why the Sharī'ah has forbidden this and it is stated in Ḥadīth that when a man and a woman are alone, the third with them is the devil.

Listening to Music

Music and songs are like poison for a person's respect and chastity. The effects of songs and music on the mind and heart are extremely dangerous and the words of songs create passion and excitement in the hearts, which then creates a desire for sins and corruption.

Allāh ﷻ has stated:

وَمِنَ النَّاسِ مَنْ يَّشْتَرِيْ لَهْوَ الْحَدِيْثِ لِيُضِلَّ عَنْ سَبِيْلِ اللّٰهِ بِغَيْرِ عِلْمٍ ۖ وَّيَتَّخِذَهَا هُزُوًا ۚ
أُولٰٓئِكَ لَهُمْ عَذَابٌ مُّهِيْنٌ

And some people buy words of play, in order to mislead from Allah's path, without knowledge; and to make it an article of mockery; for them is a disgraceful punishment.

(Sūrah Luqmān, 31: 6)

In short, Allāh ﷻ does not only dislike those who commit evil acts, but He ﷻ also dislikes those who propagate and spread evil and gives them the news of a disgraceful punishment.

He ﷻ has also stated:

إِنَّ الَّذِيْنَ يُحِبُّوْنَ أَنْ تَشِيْعَ الْفَاحِشَةُ فِي الَّذِيْنَ اٰمَنُوْا لَهُمْ عَذَابٌ أَلِيْمٌ ۙ
فِي الدُّنْيَا وَالْاٰخِرَةِ

Indeed those who wish that slander should spread among the Muslims – for them is a painful punishment in this world and in the Hereafter; and Allāh knows, and you do not know.

(Sūrah al-Nūr, 24: 19)

In terms of our societies, on the one hand we have rules, guidelines and regulations from the Qur'ān and Sunnah, whilst on the other we have free thinking parents with Western ideals and a love for the non-Islamic cultures. We have to decide which of these is more important to us.

However, before we decide, we must remember that on the Day of Judgement, we will be present in the Court of Allāh and the scene there has been mentioned in the following words in the Qur'ān:

يُنَبَّؤُا الْإِنْسَانُ يَوْمَئِذٍ بِمَا قَدَّمَ وَأَخَّرَ

On that day, man will be informed of all what he sent ahead and left behind.

(Sūrah al-Qiyāmah, 75: 13)

On that day, every soul shall be worried about itself. People will not worry about their families, friends or loved ones. According to the verses of Sūrah al-'Abas, on that day a man will run from his brother, his mother, his father, his wife and his children. A time will come upon all people on that day when they will not worry about anyone but themselves.

However, during this frightening time, there will be a group of people whose faces will be sparkling with happiness. The winds of peace and security will be blowing over them and they will be shaded by the Throne of the Almighty. It has been reported in Ṣaḥīḥ al-Bukhārī and Ṣaḥīḥ al-Muslim on the authority of Sayyidunā Abū Hurairah ﵁ that the Prophet ﷺ said:

"There are seven whom Allāh will shade in His Shade on the Day when there is no shade except His Shade: a just ruler; a youth who grew up in the worship of Allāh ﷻ; a man whose heart is attached to the Mosques; two men who love each other for Allāh's sake, meeting for that and parting upon that; a man who is called by a woman of beauty and position (for illegal intercourse), but he says, 'I fear Allāh'; a man who gives in charity and hides it, such that his left hand does not know what his right hand gives in charity; and a man who remembered Allāh in private and so his eyes shed tears." (Ṣaḥīḥ al-Bukhārī, Vol. 2, Pg. 111)

Damage Caused by Immodesty

It is in the nature of a person to want the society and community that he lives in to be peaceful, safe and pure. It is the desire of every intelligent person that he himself and his children are safeguarded from immodesty and indecency because natural human instinct desires respect, honour and chastity. If we look around us, we will realise how far removed we are from the modest and safe communities that we should have established. Indecency and immodesty are running rampant in our streets, communities, towns and cities. The devil has been busy trying since day one, however his attacks did not work on the people of previous generations. Unfortunately, him and his helpers have now achieved considerable success in this regard. Allāh ﷻ states:

اَلشَّيْطٰنُ يَعِدُكُمُ الْفَقْرَ وَيَأْمُرُكُمْ بِالْفَحْشَآءِ

The devil scares you of poverty and bids you to the shameful;

(Sūrah al-Baqarah, 2: 268)

Almighty Allāh ﷻ also states:

قُلْ تَعَالَوْا اَتْلُ مَا حَرَّمَ رَبُّكُمْ عَلَيْكُمْ اَلَّا تُشْرِكُوْا بِهٖ شَيْئًا وَّ بِالْوَالِدَيْنِ اِحْسَانًا ۚ
وَلَا تَقْتُلُوْٓا اَوْلَادَكُمْ مِّنْ اِمْلَاقٍ نَحْنُ نَرْزُقُكُمْ وَاِيَّاهُمْ وَلَا تَقْرَبُوا الْفَوَاحِشَ
مَا ظَهَرَ مِنْهَا وَمَا بَطَنَ ۚ وَلَا تَقْتُلُوا النَّفْسَ الَّتِيْ حَرَّمَ اللّٰهُ اِلَّا بِالْحَقِّ
ذٰلِكُمْ وَصّٰكُمْ بِهٖ لَعَلَّكُمْ تَعْقِلُوْنَ

Say, "Come – so that I may recite to you what your Lord has forbidden for you that 'Do not ascribe any partner to Him and be good to parents; and do not kill your children because of poverty; We shall provide sustenance for all – you and them; and do not approach lewd things, the open among them or concealed; and do not unjustly kill any life which Allāh has made sacred; this is the command to you, so that you may have sense."

(Sūrah al-An'ām, 6: 151)

At another place, He ﷻ states:

قُلْ اِنَّمَا حَرَّمَ رَبِّيَ الْفَوَاحِشَ مَا ظَهَرَ مِنْهَا وَمَا بَطَنَ وَالْاِثْمَ وَالْبَغْيَ بِغَيْرِ الْحَقِّ وَاَنْ
تُشْرِكُوْا بِاللّٰهِ مَا لَمْ يُنَزِّلْ بِهٖ سُلْطٰنًا وَّاَنْ تَقُوْلُوْا عَلَى اللّٰهِ مَا لَا تَعْلَمُوْنَ

Say, "My Lord has forbidden the indecencies, the apparent among them and the hidden, and sin and wrongful excesses, and forbidden that you ascribe partners with Allāh for which He has not sent down any proof, and forbidden that you say things concerning Allāh of which you do not have knowledge."

(Sūrah al-A'rāf, 7: 33)

Allāh ﷻ has given good news to those who avoid large sins and avoid indecency and shamelessness:

اَلَّذِيْنَ يَجْتَنِبُوْنَ كَبٰٓئِرَ الْاِثْمِ وَالْفَوَاحِشَ اِلَّا اللَّمَمَ ؕ اِنَّ رَبَّكَ وَاسِعُ الْمَغْفِرَةِ ؕ
هُوَ اَعْلَمُ بِكُمْ اِذْ اَنْشَاَكُمْ مِّنَ الْاَرْضِ وَاِذْ اَنْتُمْ اَجِنَّةٌ فِيْ بُطُوْنِ اُمَّهٰتِكُمْ ۚ
فَلَا تُزَكُّوْٓا اَنْفُسَكُمْ ؕ هُوَ اَعْلَمُ بِمَنِ اتَّقٰى

Those who avoid the cardinal sins and lewdness, except that they approached it and refrained; indeed your Lord's mercy is limitless; He knows you very well – since He has created you from clay, and when you were foetuses in your mothers' wombs; therefore do not, on your own, claim yourselves to be clean; He well knows who are the pious.

(Sūrah al-Najm, 53: 32)

For those who indulge in cardinal sins, He ﷻ has stated:

وَلَا تَقْرَبُوا الزِّنٰٓى اِنَّهٗ كَانَ فَاحِشَةً ؕ وَسَآءَ سَبِيْلًا

And do not approach adultery – it is indeed a shameful deed; and a very evil way.

(Sūrah Banī Isrā'īl, 17: 32)

Almighty Allāh ﷻ also sates:

اِنَّ الَّذِيْنَ يُحِبُّوْنَ اَنْ تَشِيْعَ الْفَاحِشَةُ فِى الَّذِيْنَ اٰمَنُوْا لَهُمْ عَذَابٌ اَلِيْمٌ فِى الدُّنْيَا وَ
الْاٰخِرَةِ ؕ وَاللّٰهُ يَعْلَمُ وَاَنْتُمْ لَا تَعْلَمُوْنَ ۝١٩ وَلَوْلَا فَضْلُ اللّٰهِ عَلَيْكُمْ وَرَحْمَتُهٗ وَاَنَّ اللّٰهَ
رَءُوْفٌ رَّحِيْمٌ ۝٢٠

Indeed those who wish that slander should spread among the Muslims – for them is a painful punishment in this world and in the Hereafter; and Allāh knows, and you do not know. And were it not for Allāh's Munificence and His Mercy upon you, and that Allāh is forgiving, most Merciful – you would have tasted its outcome.

(Sūrah al-Nūr, 24: 19-20)

Condemnation of Obscenity and Indecency in Aḥādīth

The blessed life of the beloved Prophet ﷺ is the best example for us. The following is some of what is reported in books of Aḥādīth in relation to his blessed character and morals.

Sayyidunā 'Abdullāh bin 'Umar ؓ reports that the Prophet ﷺ was not indecent, nor did he partake in indecent acts. He ﷺ has stated, "The most beloved person to me is he who has the best moral character." (Ṣaḥīḥ al-Bukhārī, Vol. 5, Pg. 28)

The following is reported in a Ḥadīth narrated by Sayyidunā 'Abdullāh ibn Mas'ūd ؓ who narrated that the Prophet ﷺ said, "No one likes to be praised more than Allāh ﷻ does which is why He has praised Himself, and there is no one more modest than Allāh ﷻ, which is why He has made indecent acts unlawful." (Ṣaḥīḥ al-Muslim, Vol. 4, Pg. 2113)

Sayyidunā Abū Hurairah ؓ narrates that the Prophet ﷺ said, "Modesty is a part of faith and faith takes a person into Paradise. Indecency is unjust and injustice takes a person into the fire." (Jāmi' al-Tirmidhī, Vol. 3, Pg. 433)

This indecency has also been mentioned in another manner in the following Ḥadīth. Sayyidunā Abū Hurairah ؓ narrates that the Prophet ﷺ said, "There are two types of the people of hell that I have not yet seen. One group is women who are clothed yet naked, walking in an enticing manner. They mislead others and are astray themselves. They have something on their heads that looks like the humps of camels, leaning to one side. They will never enter Paradise or even smell its fragrance, although its fragrance can be detected from such and such a distance." (Ṣaḥīḥ al-Muslim, Vol. 3, Pg. 168)

Even though it is women who have been condemned in this Ḥadīth, however, in reality it is condemnation of a behaviour (by both men and women) which is adopted in order to entice the opposite sex into committing adultery. It has been clearly stated in this Ḥadīth that there are indecent and immoral women who are themselves astray and are the means for misleading others. If this trait is also found in men then they are also deserving of condemnation. For example, if an immoral man entices women, talks to them in an indecent manner, tries to use his authority or wealth to convince them to commit unlawful acts, then he would also be included amongst those who have been condemned in this Ḥadīth. He also will not enter Paradise, nor will he smells its fragrance.

It is not only women who have restrictions placed on them. Rather, men have been ordered to avoid certain acts and certain situations. Ḥaḍrat 'Uqbah bin 'Āmir 🙼 narrates that the Prophet 🙼 said, "Avoid going to women in private." A person from the Anṣār asked, "O Prophet of Allāh! What is the order for a brother-in-law?" The Prophet 🙼 said, "(Meeting) the brother-in-law (in private) is death." (Ṣaḥīḥ al-Muslim, Vol. 4, Pg. 1711)

Ḥaḍrat 'Urwah 🙼 narrates that Sayyidah 'Āisha Ṣiddīqa 🙼 told him the manner that women would pledge allegiance to the Prophet. She stated that when the Prophet 🙼 would accept an oath of allegiance (Bay'at) from women, he would not shake hands with them, he would only ask them to say it verbally. The Prophet 🙼 would then say, "Go, I have accepted your pledge." (Ṣaḥīḥ al-Muslim, Vol. 3, Pg. 1489)

Explanation of Indecency

A question arises, "What exactly constitutes indecency?"

Every act which is done to obtain unlawful bodily pleasures; or if any part of the body is used in any manner to arouse sexual emotions or seek sexual pleasure, this constitutes indecency and shamelessness.

It should be remembered that adultery and sodomy are explicitly indecent acts. However, all those acts which take a person towards committing adultery are also included in the list of indecent acts. Therefore, without a lawful Islamic reason, the following are also included in the list of indecent and shameless acts – fondling, kissing, cuddling, touching, hugging, looking at another person's private parts, listening to shameless words, listening to indecent music or songs, using the hands to obtain sexual pleasure, busying the tongue with indecent words and thinking of shameless or indecent things.

The Qur'ān has mentioned adultery as being a shameless and evil act:

وَلَا تَقْرَبُوا الزِّنٰۤی اِنَّهٗ کَانَ فَاحِشَةً ؕ وَسَآءَ سَبِیْلًا

And do not approach adultery – it is indeed a shameful deed; and a very evil way.

(Sūrah Banī Isrā'īl, 17: 32)

Almighty Allāh ﷻ also states:

وَالَّذِیْنَ لَا یَدْعُوْنَ مَعَ اللّٰهِ اِلٰـهًا اٰخَرَ وَلَا یَقْتُلُوْنَ النَّفْسَ الَّتِیْ حَرَّمَ اللّٰهُ اِلَّا بِالْحَقِّ وَلَا
یَزْنُوْنَ ۚ وَمَنْ یَّفْعَلْ ذٰلِکَ یَلْقَ اَثَامًا

And those who do not worship any other deity along with Allāh, and do not unjustly kill any living thing which Allāh has forbidden, nor commit adultery; and whoever does this will receive punishment

(Sūrah al-Furqān, 25: 68)

اَلزَّانِيَةُ وَالزَّانِيْ فَاجْلِدُوْا كُلَّ وَاحِدٍ مِّنْهُمَا مِائَةَ جَلْدَةٍ ۪

وَّلَا تَاْخُذْكُمْ بِهِمَا رَاْفَةٌ فِيْ دِيْنِ اللّٰهِ

The adulteress and the adulterer – punish each one of them with a hundred lashes; and may you not have pity on them in the religion to Allāh;

(Sūrah al-Nūr, 24; 2)

اَلزَّانِيْ لَا يَنْكِحُ اِلَّا زَانِيَةً اَوْ مُشْرِكَةً ۫ وَّالزَّانِيَةُ لَا يَنْكِحُهَاۤ اِلَّا زَانٍ اَوْ مُشْرِكٌ ۚ

وَ حُرِّمَ ذٰلِكَ عَلَى الْمُؤْمِنِيْنَ

The adulterer shall not marry except an adulteress or a polytheist woman, and none shall marry an adulteress except an adulterer or a polytheist; and this is forbidden for the believers

(Sūrah al-Nūr, 24; 2)

In the early days of Islām, it was forbidden to marry an adulteress, but this order was later rescinded. (Khazāin al-'Irfān)

The Prophet ﷺ was asked, "What is the worst sin?" He replied,

أَنْ تَجْعَلَ لِلّٰهِ نِدًّا وَهُوَ خَلَقَكَ . قُلْتُ ثُمَّ أَيٌّ قَالَ أَنْ تَقْتُلَ وَلَدَكَ مِنْ أَجْلِ أَنْ يَطْعَمَ

مَعَكَ . قُلْتُ ثُمَّ أَيٌّ قَالَ أَنْ تُزَانِيَ حَلِيلَةَ جَارِكَ

"To associate partners with Allāh ﷻ, even though it is He who created you." He was asked, "What about after that?" The Prophet ﷺ replied, "To kill your own child for fear of poverty." He was asked, "What about after that?" He ﷺ replied, "Committing adultery with your neighbours wife."

(Ṣaḥīḥ al-Bukhārī, Vol. 9, Pg. 2)

In another Ḥadīth it is stated, "When an adulterer commits adultery, he is not a believer and when a thief is committing burglary, he is not a believer and when an alcoholic is drinking alcohol, he is not a believer." (Sunan Ibn Mājah, Vol. 2, Pg. 1298)

It is also stated in a Ḥadīth that, "When a person commits adultery, faith leaves him and hovers above him. When he stops, his faith returns to him."

In yet another Ḥadīth, it is stated, "There are three (types of) people whom Allāh ﷻ will not speak to on the Day of Resurrection, nor will He purify them, nor look at them, and they will have a painful punishment. These are: An aged man who commits adultery, a ruler who lies and an arrogant poor person." (Ṣaḥīḥ al-Muslim, Vol. 1, Pg. 102)

Sayyidunā Abū Hurairah ؓ narrates that the Prophet ﷺ said, "Verily, Allāh ﷻ has written for the son of Ādam his portion of adultery which he will inevitably commit; the adultery of the eyes is a lustful look, the adultery of the tongue is lustful speech, and the soul hopes and lusts for what the private parts will fulfil or deny." (Ṣaḥīḥ al-Muslim, Vol. 4, Pg. 2046)

Indecent Material

Indecent material refers to any publication, picture, photograph, video, music, words, gestures, jokes, nudity or any other manner in which sexual organs or sexual acts are seen or spoken about, which arouses sexual passion or gives sexual satisfaction.

For any matter or material to be considered indecent, the following conditions must be present:
Looking at the sexual organs of someone who is not your lawful spouse. The intention must be to arouse sexual passion or achieve sexual pleasure. Therefore, if literature is produced for medical, legal or other lawful purposes, it will not be considered indecent.

Propagating Indecent Material

Any kind of indecent act is an extremely evil deed. However, it becomes even more evil when the indecent act is publicised and boasted about. For example, committing adultery is a despicable act but to publicise it on Facebook etc. could be the means for many others to be misguided. On the one hand, it is important to protect one's self from indecency, whilst propagating it, publicising it and spreading it through various social media platforms is also a great sin.

Propagating indecent material means to advertise or publicise any sexual act or sexual material to others without a valid reason. Therefore, to pass any sexual material onto others to seek sexual pleasure, to make money, to pass time or simply to please others is considered as propagating indecent material; regardless if that material is written, spoken, a photograph, video, audio or in any other form.

Propagating Indecent Material Forbidden

Ḥaḍrat Abū Sa'īd al-Khudrī ﷺ narrates that the Prophet ﷺ said, "The worst of people in status in the Sight of Allāh ﷻ on the Day of Judgement will be the man who has sexual relations with his wife and then tells others about his sexual relations with her." (Ṣaḥīḥ al-Muslim)

As you can see, it is even forbidden to talk about the lawful sexual relations between a husband and wife, let alone talk about indecent and unlawful relations which may take place. Therefore, whether it is literature, SMS, text message, Facebook, email, newspaper, magazine, television or any other form, it is explicitly forbidden to produce or pass on to others any form of indecent material. Allāh ﷻ has given strict warning of grave punishment in this world and the hereafter for those who do this.

Indecency and the Media

In the current era, since the arrival of social media, news and information travels around the globe in seconds. Facebook, Twitter, Whatsapp and other social media platforms pass information to hundreds of thousands of people with a single click of the mouse. This can also be done through SMS, emails and various other messenger platforms.

Regardless of which form of media is used, it is able to send information from one place to one another very quickly. However, it does not differentiate between what is correct and what is incorrect. Therefore, the information could be accurate or it could be false. When sharing any kind of news, picture, quote, joke, movie clip, book or article etc. on social media, electronic media or print media, care should be taken to ensure that what is being shared is accurate and is not indecent or immoral.

In complete opposition to the guidance given by the Qur'ān and the Ḥadīth, nowadays the media – under the influence of the West – is giving prominence to and spreading many forms of indecency and nudity. This includes news programs on TV, dramas, musicals, films, newspapers and magazines containing pictures of semi-nude people and short books and novels which contain indecent stories. In the same manner, the Internet and various websites have opened the floodgates of indecency and nudity and placed them in every home and in every bedroom. Indecent material and pornography is available with a single click on a PC, laptop, mobile phone, iPad or tablet. In spite of the guidance and strict warnings given by Islām, people in general, and youngsters in particular, are polluting the eyes and ears with indecent material and filling their minds with visions of nudity and pornography.

On the other hand, our people are not merely satisfied with viewing the indecent material themselves, rather they are full participants in spreading and propagating it. When a youngster receives a nude picture, indecent SMS, rude joke, pornographic movie clip, or any other indecent material, he feels a sense of pride in forwarding it to others. In this manner, not only is he committing a sin himself but he is also being the means for others to commit sin. This falls into the category of 'propagating indecent material', which has been severely reprimanded in the Qur'ān.

How to Avoid Shamelessness and Indecency

1) Youngsters who are unmarried and are involved in any form of indecency should, if they are able, get married immediately. This has been mentioned in the Qur'ān in the following words:

وَاَنْكِحُوا الْاَيَامٰى مِنْكُمْ وَالصّٰلِحِيْنَ مِنْ عِبَادِكُمْ وَاِمَآئِكُمْ ۚ اِنْ يَّكُوْنُوْا

فُقَرَآءَ يُغْنِهِمُ اللّٰهُ مِنْ فَضْلِهٖ ۚ وَاللّٰهُ وَاسِعٌ عَلِيْمٌ

And enjoin in marriage those among you who are not married (males or females), and your deserving slaves and bondwomen; if they are poor, Allāh will make them wealthy by His munificence; and Allāh is Most Capable, All Knowing.

(Sūrah al-Nūr, 24: 32)

It has been mentioned quite clearly in this verse that if a person is not getting married due to his financial situation or he does not have enough wealth, then Allāh ﷻ, through His Grace, will make him wealthy. The following verse states:

وَلْيَسْتَعْفِفِ الَّذِيْنَ لَا يَجِدُوْنَ نِكَاحًا حَتّٰى يُغْنِيَهُمُ اللّٰهُ مِنْ فَضْلِهٖ

And those who do not have the means to get married must keep chaste till Allāh provides them the resources by His munificence;

(Sūrah al-Nūr, 24: 33)

In this verse those who have absolutely no wealth are being given guidance and instructions to wait until such a time when Allāh ﷻ will make them capable. However, it is very clear from these verses that those people who are unable to get married for any reason are not being told that they should partake in adultery, fornication or any form of indecency in order to fulfil their sexual desires. Rather, they are told quite clearly that they should remain chaste and protect their dignity, purity and honour. Guidance for how to remain chaste has been mentioned in a Ḥadīth which states that those who are single should get married, or if they are unable to get married they should fast, because fasting reduces sexual desires. It is stated in a Ḥadīth:

Ḥaḍrat Ibrahim ؒ and Ḥaḍrat 'Alqamah ؒ report that they were walking with Ḥaḍrat 'Abdullāh ibn Mas'ūd ؓ and he said, "I was walking with the Prophet ﷺ when he said, "The one who has the ability to pay *Mahr* should get married because that lowers a person's gaze and safeguards the private parts from committing adultery. And those who do not have the ability should fast, as that will be a shield for them." (Ṣaḥīḥ al-Bukhārī, Vol. 3, Pg. 26)

2) Those people who are married and still indulge in indecencies should have some respect for their spouse and only engage in sexual relations with their spouse. This will provide comfort, peace and satisfaction in the heart which pornography or indecent material can never provide. It is stated in a Ḥadīth:

Sayyidunā Abū Hurairah ﷺ narrates that the Prophet ﷺ saw a woman and then went to his wife Ḥaḍrat Zainab ﷺ as she was tanning leather. He ﷺ then had relations with his wife and then returned to his Companions and said, "The woman advances and retires in the shape of a devil, so when one of you sees a woman (and is attracted to her beauty), he should come to his wife, for that will repel what he feels in his heart." (Ṣaḥīḥ al-Muslim, Vol. 2, Pg. 1021)

3) Safeguard the eyes and always have pure thoughts and this is only possible if you are in an environment which is free from indecency and indecent materials. Therefore, use the internet only when it is absolutely necessary. Computers, laptops and other devices should be used in public where it is easy for others to see what you are doing. Doing this is an easy way to avoid indecency and indecent materials.

4) Precautionary measures should be taken at places where there is a strong possibility of coming into contact with members of the opposite sex. Firstly the eyes should be protected and kept pure; the body and especially the private parts should be well covered; no step should be taken which could incite excitement or sexual desire. This guidance applies to both males and females.

5) Give yourself a fine or penalty for carrying out any act of indecency or shamelessness. Meaning if you commit any act which is indecent then you should pay a monetary or physical fine. For example, you can stipulate that even after trying your best you visit an indecent website,

then you will give a percentage of your wages in the path of Allāh ﷻ. If you happen to slip up then enforce the penalty strictly. Another possibility is that if you slip up, you will fast or you will pray ten raka'āt voluntary prayers. However, care must be taken when establishing what the penalty will be. It must not be so small that it makes no difference and must not be so high that it is difficult to act upon.

In spite of all this guidance, it is still possible to make an error and commit a sin. Therefore, if an act is committed which goes against modesty, you should keep control of your anger and nerves. At times like this the devil tells you that you have committed the sin now and are upset so go ahead and commit this sin completely and openly. Do not be disheartened after committing any sin. Immediately after the sin has been committed, turn to Allāh ﷻ. The method of doing this is to perform two rakā'at prayer and seek forgiveness from Allāh ﷻ. Or seek forgiveness with the tongue and make a firm intention and promise to not commit that sin again in the future. If this promise is broken time and again for any reason then forgiveness should be sought after each slip up. This is because if a person seeks forgiveness there is a possibility that he will eventually give up the bad deed. However, if repenting and seeking forgiveness are given up, then there is no possibility of giving up the bad deed.

6) Keep yourself busy with as many positive and beneficial activities as possible. Study Islamic books, keep the company of pious and religious people, help the poor and needy and participate in social programmes which benefit the community at large.

7) Completely avoid films, dramas, novels, magazines and websites which arouse passion and sexual desire.

8) Keep the body healthy and active by playing sports or doing regular exercise.

9) During times of any difficulty or confusion, do not be scared or embarrassed of seeking advice from knowledgeable and experienced people.

Avoiding Indecent Material

Looking at or using any indecent material is in itself a grave sin. Therefore, all attempts should be made to avoid indecency and guard yourself against any form of indecent material. Along with this, it should never be forwarded or shared with others. The following is guidance in this regard.

Muslim producers, editors, writers, artists, cameramen and their assistants who partake in spreading indecency as part of their job and profession should realise that they are embroiled in a number of sins. The first is that they themselves are partaking in indecency; secondly, they are propagating it; thirdly, they are earning the sins of countless people who are being misguided; and fourthly, they are earning unlawful money. If the punishment for merely propagating and spreading indecent material is the fire of hell, then the punishment for all of the sins that have been mentioned cannot even be comprehended. To avoid this, they should seek forgiveness from Allāh ﷻ and supplicate to Him to find lawful and pure sustenance. It is stated in the Qur'ān that a person who fears Allāh ﷻ is given sustenance by Him from places and in ways that he cannot even imagine.

Those people who share indecent material through Facebook and other social, electronic and print media forums, should remember the warnings and threats of the fire that are given in Sūrah al-Nūr. It is an expensive and unprofitable transaction whereby in order to please people for a moment, you are purchasing the fire of hell for yourself.

Sometimes it so happens that the message which is being shared is not indecent, but there is a hidden message in it which happens to be indecent and immoral. Therefore, before sharing any picture, movie, quote, joke or any other thing, care should be taken to ensure that it does not contain any kind of indecency or immorality. If this is the case, then it should not be shared.

Islām has given us the foundations for building the best societies and has restricted all things which can ruin and destroy communities, cultures and societies. Shamelessness, indecency and immorality are diseases which can destroy societies in a matter of moments. This is why Islām has placed restrictions on all such things.

Examples of Immodesty in Society

The effects of Western culture and ideals which have entered our homes through movies and social media are evident in a number of ways in our society. The environment of shamelessness and immodesty, which until yesterday was improper and inappropriate in our eyes, is now considered an important and integral part of our culture. Some of our people even consider it a sign of advancement and success, even though we are all well aware of the damaging effects that it has caused. Some areas of improvement are being mentioned so that we can ponder on them and try to implement them into our lives and communities.

Women Wearing Tight Clothing

The types of clothing which have taken hold in our societies in the name of fashion and how much of the body they actually cover, is not hidden from anybody with any kind of intelligence. In spite of this, not only is there no communal effort to rectify this, individual efforts are nowhere near where they need to be. In the past, clothing was based on Islamic morals and clothing was used to cover and hide the body. This responsibility has now been taken on by fashion designers. Such is the state of *niqābs* that the whole point of wearing a *niqāb* is defeated. *Niqābs* used to be worn so that women would be safeguarded from the glances and gaze of *ghayr maḥram* men. Nowadays, *niqābs* are being designed in such a manner that a man's attention and focus is automatically drawn towards it and the women wearing them. The evil result of this is being seen in this world whilst the punishment in the hereafter will be unbearable.

Sayyidunā Abū Hurairah ﵁ narrates that the Prophet ﷺ said:

صِنْفَانِ مِنْ اَهْلِ النَّارِ لَمْ اَرَهُمَا، قَوْمٌ مَعَهُمْ سِيَاطٌ كَاَذْنَابِ الْبَقَرِ يَضْرِبُوْنَ بِهَا النَّاسَ وَنِسَاءٌ كَاسِيَاتٌ عَارِيَاتٌ مُمِيْلَاتٌ مَائِلَاتٌ رُءُوْسُهُنَّ كَاَسْنِمَةِ الْبُخْتِ الْمَائِلَةِ لَا يَدْخُلْنَ الْجَنَّةَ وَلَا يَجِدْنَ رِيحَهَا وَاِنَّ رِيحَهَا لَيُوْجَدُ مِنْ مَسِيْرَةِ كَذَا وَكَذَا

There are two types of people who will enter the fire, whom I have not (as yet) seen; Men having whips similar to ox-tails with which they will beat people, and (secondly) women who will be dressed yet appear to

be naked. They will seduce men and be inclined towards them. Their heads will be like the swaying humps of bacterial camels. They will neither enter paradise, nor smell its fragrance, even though its fragrance can be smelt from such and such distance.

(Ṣaḥīḥ al-Muslim, Vol. 3, Pg. 1680)

In this era and culture of fashion the state of women's clothing and even *niqābs* is such that even when they are clothed, the outline and shape of their bodies can be clearly seen. They have weird and strange hairstyles which they leave uncovered and display it to the world. Firstly, the Prophet ﷺ described them as dwellers of the fire who are unlike any other dwellers and secondly, he ﷺ has stated that these women will be so far from Paradise that they will not even smell its fragrance.

Those women who wear pants, trousers, leggings, thin clothes, thin head coverings and other clothing which do not cover the body properly should take warning from this and rectify themselves.

Laughing and Joking with Brother-In-Law and Sister-In-Law

One of the illnesses which is very common in our communities is that covering oneself in front of the husband's brother is considered old fashioned. It is considered appropriate to spend time alone and laugh and joke with a brother-in-law or sister-in-law. Sometimes this conversation becomes indecent and contains inappropriate words and phrases. It does not then take long for these words to be turned into action by these 'free-thinking' and 'modern' brother-in-laws and sister-in-laws. The evil effects of this are before our very eyes and yet still there is no effort being made to stop this evil and inappropriate practice.

Remember! The brother of one's husband or the husband of one's sister is a *ghayr maḥram* male. Laughing, joking and spending time alone with them is a far cry, it is not even permissible to speak with them unless it is absolutely necessary.

Ḥaḍrat 'Uqbah bin 'Āmir رضي الله عنه narrates that the Prophet ﷺ said:

إِيَّاكُمْ وَالدُّخُولَ عَلَى النِّسَاءِ

Avoid being in the company of women.

Upon hearing this, one of the Companions asked, "What is the order for a brother-in-law?" The Prophet ﷺ said, "(Meeting) the brother-in-law (in private) is death (for the woman)."

In this Ḥadīth it has been forbidden for a man to be alone with a *ghayr maḥram* female. It has been specifically stated that a man should especially avoid being alone with the wife of his brother.

Having Permission to Enter the Home Freely

Friendship is a good thing but it is better if it is kept outside the home. *Ghayr maḥram* males, even if they are very good friends, can be a source of strife and tribulation in the home. Many people allow their friends to come freely in and out of their homes. The women of the homes also have close and direct communications with these friends. Undoubtedly this is impermissible according to Islām and we are all aware of the damage and devastation this causes. It is essential to have friends but do not take the rules and orders regarding friends lightly. Fulfil the rights of friendship outside the home otherwise you will be responsible for the devastation that it causes.

Incorrect Use of Electronic Media

Electronic media has played a huge role in spreading and giving rise to immorality and shamelessness in our societies. The programmes which are shown on television, such as dramas, movies and even adverts, are full of indecency and shamelessness. It is easy for the minds of youngsters to turn towards these things after watching such shows and programmes. In this instance, it is the responsibility of parents to keep an eye on their young and teenage children. They must protect their children and not allow them to watch such shows on television which will contaminate and destroy their minds, morals and character.

Mobile Phones and Internet

Where mobile phones and the internet help in a lot of important matters, they also play an important role in destroying character, morals and the mind-set of youngsters. Some of the biggest evils of the internet are indecent music, pornographic movies, nudity, shamelessness and immodesty. It fulfils the desires of the eyes and the ears which is why people are in love with it. The Sharī'ah does not forbid taking advantage of and using new technology, however it is essential to keep that use within the limits set by the Sharī'ah. New technology has opened new doors of evils and sins but the Qur'ān is still proclaiming loudly:

إِنَّ بَطْشَ رَبِّكَ لَشَدِيدٌ

Indeed the seizure of your Lord is very severe.

(Sūrah al-Burūj, 85: 12)

At another place, the Holy Qur'ān states:

إِنَّ السَّمْعَ وَالْبَصَرَ وَالْفُؤَادَ كُلُّ أُولَٰئِكَ كَانَ عَنْهُ مَسْئُولًا

Indeed the ear, and the eye, and the heart – each of these will be questioned.

(Sūrah Banī Isrā'īl, 17: 36)

Facebook and Whatsapp

Islām placed restrictions on men speaking to *ghayr maḥram* women and women speaking to *ghayr maḥram* men and people generally abided by these restrictions. However, nowadays Facebook, Whatsapp and similar extravagances have increased the number of ways in which a person can commit sins and disobey the orders of Islām. Looking at *ghayr maḥram* members of the opposite sex on Facebook, becoming their friend, spending hours chatting with them and then contacting them through Whatsapp and gradually moving towards sins has become very common. The greatest injustice is that this is not even considered wrong or evil by society. Rather, the reality is that a person who does not have Facebook and Whatsapp is looked at with contempt by others. A person should not think that having a password on his phone or deleting his chat history makes him safe. Allāh ﷻ is aware of every action of each and every one of us. Based on His orders, the Angels are busy writing down what we do every second of the day and on the Day of Judgement, in front of everybody, the following order will be given:

اِقۡرَاۡ كِتٰبَكَ ؕ كَفٰى بِنَفۡسِكَ الۡيَوۡمَ عَلَيۡكَ حَسِيۡبًا ؕ ﴿۱۴﴾ مَنِ اهۡتَدٰى فَاِنَّمَا يَهۡتَدِىۡ لِنَفۡسِهٖ ۚ
وَمَنۡ ضَلَّ فَاِنَّمَا يَضِلُّ عَلَيۡهَا ؕ وَلَا تَزِرُ وَازِرَةٌ وِّزۡرَ اُخۡرٰى ؕ وَمَا كُنَّا مُعَذِّبِيۡنَ
حَتّٰى نَبۡعَثَ رَسُوۡلًا ﴿۱۵﴾

It will be said, "Read your ledger; this day you are sufficient to take your own account." Whoever came to guidance, has come for his own good; and whoever went astray, has strayed for his own ruin; and no burdened soul will bear another's burden; and We never punish until We have sent a Noble Messenger

(Sūrah Banī Isrā'īl, 17: 14-15)

Just imagine! How will we read the accounts of all the immodesty and indecency which we have committed?

Final Word

Teach Children Modesty From an Early Age

As young children grow, they should be taught about the need to keep (the body) covered. They should be reminded about the difference between *maḥram* and *ghayr maḥram* people (as explained in the Qur'ān and Ḥadīth) on a regular basis. This is because the more chances there are of an illness, the more precautions need to be taken. Nudity, immodesty, mixed gatherings of men and women, shameless conversations, clothing which does not cover the private parts, adopting shamelessness and immorality and calling it fashion – these are all illnesses which have no limit as to how far they will go. In order to make a stand against these illnesses and protect ourselves from them, it is necessary to surround our children with an Islamic spirit when they are growing up. It is essential to give this the importance that it deserves because society is getting used to these evils and there seems to be nothing to stop us from falling into the same pit.

From a young age it should be arranged for young boys and young girls to play separately from each other. Nurseries and primary schools are generally coeducation, where boys and girls are taught together. From the start of education boys and girls should be taught separately, or if that is not possible, children should not be sent to such places. If that is not a possibility, then before sending children to such places of education they should be made aware of protecting their eyes, ears and hearts. They should be taught that Allāh ﷻ sees every large and small thing that they do and think and that all forms of immodesty and shamelessness have been declared unlawful by Him.

Those children who are brought up in an Islamic environment and have been taught to be punctual with their obligatory prayers will not have any difficulty in understanding and acting upon what they are told. Young girls should be taught about Islamic clothing from the age of three. Rather, they should not be dressed in any clothing, even at that young age, which is against Islamic teachings. In the same way, in the home and outside the home, they should be constantly reminded about the difference between permissible (*Maḥram*) and impermissible (*Ghayr maḥram*) people. In this manner, when they reach the age of 13 or 14 they will not question the need to wear a ḥijāb, jilbāb or scarf and will adopt it unquestionably.

Young boys and girls should be kept away from the television and the internet as much as possible. Young girls should be told stories about the pious women of Islām and how they kept themselves covered and modest at all times. There are many Islamic websites aimed at children and they should be encouraged to visit those instead of playing games or just passing time on the internet.

Important Point

All these restrictions which Islām has placed, as well as other orders which close the door to shamelessness and immodesty, contain countless wisdoms. If we study Aḥādīth, we will see that great emphasis is placed on staying away from and eliminating any and all forms of immodesty, indecency and shamelessness. The punishments which will be given for each act of immodesty have also been described in detail in Aḥādīth. The indecencies and their punishments which have been mentioned in detail are listed below. This should be enough to open the eyes of people with belief who have been careless and negligent to this point:

- Making the face beautiful for a *ghayr maḥram* person – The face will be black on the Day of Judgement.
- Looking at the face of a *ghayr maḥram* person with love [desire] – The face will be burnt on the Day of Judgement.
- Becoming happy and excited when seeing a *ghayr maḥram* person – The face will be branded with the fire of hell on the Day of Judgement.
- Talking with a *ghayr maḥram* person in an intimate manner – Will wake up crying on the Day of Judgement.
- Laughing and joking with a *ghayr maḥram* person – Will wake up screaming in agony on the Day of Judgement.
- Becoming happy when meeting a *ghayr maḥram* person – Will wake up sad and distressed on the Day of Judgement.
- Looking at a *ghayr maḥram* person with lust and desire – Hot iron rods will be placed in the eyes on the Day of Judgement.
- Walking to go and meet and *ghayr maḥram* person – Shackles of fire will be placed on the feet on the Day of Judgement.

- Holding hands with a *ghayr maḥram* person – The hands will be tied with handcuffs of fire on the Day of Judgement.
- Started the act of adultery by kissing a *ghayr maḥram* person on the lips – Will be dragged by the face and thrown into the fire of hell on the Day of Judgement.
- Removing clothing and exposing the private parts in front of a *ghayr maḥram* person – Will be made to wear clothing of hot tar on the Day of Judgement.
- Quenching sexual thirst with a *ghayr maḥram* person – Will wake up thirsty on the Day of Judgement.
- Becoming sexually aroused when meeting a *ghayr maḥram* person – The private parts will be set on fire on the Day of Judgement.
- Ejaculating semen from the private parts when meeting a *ghayr maḥram* person – The private parts will emit a foul odour on the Day of Judgement.
- Running the fingers through their hair of a *ghayr maḥram* person out of love and affection – Will be hung by the hair in the fire of hell on the Day of Judgement.
- Touching or kissing the breasts of a *ghayr maḥram* person – Will be hung by the breasts in the fire of hell on the Day of Judgement.
- Smelling the bodily fragrance of a *ghayr maḥram* person – A horrible and pungent smell will come from the body on the Day of Judgement.
- Sleeping on the same bed with a *ghayr maḥram* person – They will be placed together in an oven of fire on the Day of Judgement.
- Exposing the body in front of a *ghayr maḥram* person – Will be exposed and naked in front of Allāh ﷻ on the Day of Judgement.
- Hiding from people in order to commit adultery with a *ghayr maḥram* person – Will be exposed and disgraced in front of all of creation on the Day of Judgement.
- Lying to people in order to hide a relationship with a *ghayr maḥram* person – The mouth will be sealed and evidence shall be taken from the various body parts on the Day of Judgement.

- Listening to praise about one's beauty from a *ghayr maḥram* person – All people will be cursing them on the Day of Judgement.
- Greeting a *ghayr maḥram* person when meeting in private – Will be cursed by Allāh ﷻ on the Day of Judgement.
- Kissing the body of a *ghayr maḥram* person– Snakes will bite every part of the body on the Day of Judgement.
- Different parts of the body feeling pleasure when committing adultery – Scorpions will sting every part of the body on the Day of Judgement.
- Feeling control and authority over the body of a *ghayr maḥram* person – The spouse of that person will have control and authority over your good deeds on the Day of Judgement.
- Climbed on the body of a *ghayr maḥram* person – The sins of the spouse of the *ghayr maḥram* person will be placed on the head on the Day of Judgement.
- Promising lifelong friendship to a *ghayr maḥram* person – Punishment forever in the fire of hell will be promised on the Day of Judgement.
- Feeling excitement and pleasure in speaking to a *ghayr maḥram* person – Will be deprived of the pleasure of speaking to and listening to Allāh ﷻ on the Day of Judgement.

Shamelessness and indecency are considered extremely inappropriate in Islām which is why there are so many warnings and threats of punishment against each thing which could lead to them. In spite of this, there seems to be a general lack of care about this in our societies. Modern educational facilities, offices, parties, weddings and other such places and gatherings are full of immodesty and shamelessness. It is necessary for us to be anxious about this worrying trend and work towards rectifying ourselves and our communities. May Allāh ﷻ guide us all to adopt modesty in our actions and words and instil in us all the passion and desire to create homes, communities and societies filled with modesty, humility and obedience to Allāh ﷻ and His Beloved ﷺ, Āmīn.

SUNNI DAWATE ISLAMI THE WORLDWIDE ISLAMIC MOVEMENT

سنی دعوت اسلامی

نٓ وَالْقَلَمِ وَمَا يَسْطُرُونَ

وأما بنعمة ربك فحدث